given to Rae
by HOUS[

COUNSELS

COUNSELS
OF
PERFECTION

A Bahá'í Guide to Mature Living

GENEVIEVE COY

GEORGE RONALD
OXFORD

GEORGE RONALD, Publisher
46 High Street, Kidlington, Oxford OX5 2DN

The publishers wish to express their grateful thanks to the Universal House of Justice, the National Spiritual Assembly of the United States of America, and the Bahá'í Publishing Trust, London, for permission to quote from their publications.

ISBN 0 85398 079 9 (cased)
ISBN 0 85398 080 2 (paper)

Typeset by
Getset Ltd, Eynsham, Oxford
Printed in
the United States of America

CONTENTS

1	Why This Book	*page*	1
2	The Prison of Self		7
3	Strive for Gentleness and Love		22
4	Action and Achievement		35
5	The Use of Intelligence		46
6	The Use of Money		59
7	The Development of Arts and Sciences		72
8	Education in the Home		88
9	Education in Schools		101
10	Men and Women		120
11	Fairness to Yourself and Others		133
12	Consultation		144
13	Joy Gives Us Wings		154
	Bibliography		177
	References		179

To

MARGUERITE AND WILLIAM SEARS

in appreciation for the lessons in faith
they have taught me

1

WHY THIS BOOK?

BAHÁ'ÍS WHO KNOW that my field of work is psychology have often said to me, 'If one has the Bahá'í teachings, one should not need psychology.' My answer has always been, 'But don't you realize that the Bahá'í teachings are overflowing with the principles of psychology?' This answer suprises some people, perhaps because they have not read the teachings with care, or because they do not understand that psychology covers the whole science of human relationships. It is not primarily, a method of dream interpretation, nor a technique for helping a salesman to sell more goods!

When I realized that many Bahá'ís did not recognize the principles of human relationship which are so clearly stated by Bahá'u'lláh and 'Abdu'l-Bahá, I decided that when I retired I would write a book which would analyse and summarize the psychology in the Bahá'í Writings. This book is the result.

The primary duty of Bahá'ís is so to live that they *increase unity* among all mankind. This is also the purpose of many others who know that the only hope for a peaceful, stable world is to increase understanding and fellowship among all peoples.

Many of us do not realize how often our behaviour

decreases unity among our kindred, friends, and fellow-workers. When we come to an understanding of how divisive some of our actions are, we discover that we must re-form our characters. This book is primarily a set of suggestions as to how we may develop our characters in such a way that we increase the friendliness, the kindness, and the love which will bring greater unity among mankind.

> Therefore, we must strive with life and heart that day by day, our deeds may be better, our conduct more beautiful and our forbearance greater. That is to cultivate love for all the world; to attain beatific character.[1]

For Whom is this Book Written?

1. This book is written for Bahá'ís who are eager to understand themselves better, and to develop their abilities so that they may be more able to contribute to the welfare of mankind. They believe that only in this way can they do the will of God in this age.

> . . . the duty of the Bahá'ís . . . to give these principles unfoldment and application in the minds, hearts and lives of the people.[2]

2. Students of the Bahá'í Faith often ask, 'What are the Bahá'í teachings which help a person to live better day by day?' It is hoped that this book will serve as a detailed answer to that question.

3. Many others have as yet no interest in the Bahá'í teachings, but they believe in God and wish to

do His will. I have written these chapters for them, also, in the hope that they will find them helpful in their efforts to serve God and mankind.

4. Still others, who do not have a deep faith in God, may find in these pages some practical applications of psychology which they will find useful.

Purposes Served by the Quotations from the Bahá'í Writings

This book is not intended to be a compilation from the Bahá'í Writings, even though there are over two hundred quotations from Bahá'u'lláh and 'Abdu'l-Bahá. Most of these are brief. They serve a variety of purposes:

1. They may be used to introduce the topic of a chapter. For example in chapter 2, five quotations emphasize the necessity of avoiding egotism.

2. They may summarize the basic purpose of a chapter. At the end of chapter 3, six quotations point out that love of people and love of God are interdependent.

3. In many instances the purpose of the quotations is to introduce a new aspect of the topic, to carry the thought a step further. For example in chapter 9, the topic of adult education is introduced by four quotations which stress the need for man to go on learning to the end of his life.

4. It is hoped that many of the quotations may be used as a basis for discussion in a group which reads the book together. In some instances the readers may

feel that the application of a quotation which I have made is far-fetched or untrue. Discussion of such statements should bring out many of the implications of the principle stated by Bahá'u'lláh or 'Abdu'l-Bahá.

5. I hope that many Bahá'ís will turn to the sources of the quotations and will read more of the context in which the brief quotation is set. This is especially important in cases where the reader is surprised to find a given statement in the Writings. A deep student of the Faith, on reading in chapter 11 a sentence quoted from *The Hidden Words,* '. . . no man should enter the house of his friend save at his friend's pleasure . . .', said, 'I can't remember ever reading that!' One may read a sentence ten times, and only on the eleventh reading begin to understand its full meaning.

Translations

The books and Tablets (letters) of Bahá'u'lláh and 'Abdu'l-Bahá were all written in Persian or Arabic, and therefore the quality of the translation must be considered. The translations of the Writings of Bahá'u'lláh from which we quote were made by Shoghi Effendi, Guardian of the Bahá'í Faith, or under the direction of the Universal House of Justice.* We can therefore be sure of their accuracy.

In the case of the Writings of 'Abdu'l-Bahá many translators are involved. The talks given by Him in America, presented in *The Promulgation of Universal*

*Except for reference 10, Chapter 10.

Peace, were all taken down by skilled stenographers, but several translators were used. In the case of the three volumes of *Tablets of Abdul-Baha Abbas* translations were often made by Persians, who were reasonably accurate, but whose skill in written English was not too great. On the other hand, such a volume as Marzieh Gail's translation of *The Secret of Divine Civilization* is outstanding for accuracy and English style.

In quoting from the Writings it is of course necessary to follow exactly the published translation. The reader is therefore asked to be lenient toward the inadequate English which one sometimes finds, especially in the *Tablets* of 'Abdu'l-Bahá.

The Persian and Arabic languages do not use capital letters, and each translator has tended to follow his own ideas on which words to capitalize. Thus the attributes of God, such as love, mercy, and glory, are written with capitals by one translator, but not by another. The more recently published Bahá'í books tend to decrease the amount of capitalization, except when referring directly to God and His Manifestations.

Is this Book too Elementary?

Some readers will no doubt find that parts of this book seem to them too simple. They may think, 'I have always known this and practised it. Why put it into print?' But the principle that these readers find commonplace is often a new idea to others, who value having its implications stated and illustrated.

My reasons for including principles which may seem elementary are, first, they are in the Bahá'í Writings and therefore Bahá'u'lláh must have thought it necessary to state them; second, every principle included has been called to my attention by those who failed to practise it!

The light of a good character surpasseth the light of the sun and the radiance thereof. Whoso attaineth unto it is accounted as a jewel among men.[3]

Whoso ariseth, in this Day, to aid Our Cause, and summoneth to his assistance the hosts of a praiseworthy character and upright conduct, the influence flowing from such an action will, most certainly, be diffused throughout the whole world.[4]

2

THE PRISON OF SELF

IF WE WERE asked, 'Do you wish to be selfish?', most of us would answer, 'No, of course not!' But the Bahá'í idea of self-love implies a great deal more than is usually understood by the word 'selfishness'. Self-love covers all those attitudes and actions which tend to separate us from other human beings. Many of them are mentioned specifically in the Bahá'í Writings; others are present by implication. The need to avoid self-love is clearly indicated in the following passages.

O Children of Men! Know ye not why We created you all from the same dust? That no one should exalt himself over the other. Ponder at all times in your hearts how ye were created. . . .[1]

O My Servant! Free thyself from the fetters of this world, and loose thy Soul from the prison of self. Seize thy chance, for it will come to thee no more.[2]

O My Servant! Thou art even as a finely tempered sword concealed in the darkness of its sheath and its value hidden from the artificer's knowledge. Wherefore come forth from the sheath of self and desire that thy worth may be made resplendent and manifest unto all the world.[3]

This test is just as thou hast written: it removeth the rust of egotism from the mirror of the heart until the Sun of Truth may shine therein. For, no veil is greater than egotism and no matter how thin that covering may be, yet it will finally veil man entirely and prevent him from receiving a portion from the eternal bounty.[4]

If man be imbued with all good qualities but be selfish, all the other virtues will fade or pass away . . .[5]

But the human ego is so subtle that often we do not recognize that certain acts are expressions of self-love. The remainder of this chapter will analyse some of the ways in which egotism is expressed.

'I Must be First'

Our competitive culture makes it extremely difficult for a person to free himself from the cult of having to be first. Newspapers, magazines, radio, and television are filled with acclaim for the wealthiest, the most powerful, the most glamorous, the most intelligent. I may know that I am not the wealthiest person in my town, but I may comfort myself by thinking, 'Ah, but I have a larger income than my next-door neighbour', and in this way I try to make myself 'first' within my neighbourhood. A boy who is not the best reader in his class may win a 'first' for himself by becoming the most troublesome.

These strivings to be first tend to produce separateness, rather than unity and fellowship. They are ways in which an individual tries to 'exalt himself over the other'. If a man spends his energy in making the best possible use of his abilities, without worrying whether he is first, or fifth, or tenth, his accomplishment is likely to be greater than that of an equally gifted but competitive person, and, more important, he does not divide those around him by treating them as rivals.

The true Bahá'í must make every effort not to become entangled in the web of competition. He may not excuse himself on the grounds that 'it is natural to want to be first', or that 'in our society you have to be competitive'.

Blessed are the learned that pride not themselves on their attainments. . .[6]

Help him to see and recognize the truth, without esteeming yourself to be, in the least, superior to him, or to be possessed of greater endowments.[7]

We must seek no name nor fame, no ease, amplitude nor convenience. . .[8]

The second attribute of perfection is justice and impartiality. This means to have no regard for one's own personal benefits and selfish advantages, and to carry out the laws of God without the slightest concern for anything else. It means to see one's self as only one of the servants of God, the All-Possessing, and except for aspiring to spiritual distinction, never attempting to be singled out from the others.[9]

Envy, jealousy, and covetousness may be thought of as by-products of the desire to be first. Of these three the influence of envy seems to be the worst for causing unfriendly behaviour. If you have done something unkind which you then regretted, search honestly to learn whether envy may have been at the root of it.

We pray God to protect thee from the heat of jealousy and the cold of hatred.[10]

O Son of Earth! Know, verily, the heart wherein the least remnant of envy yet lingers, shall never attain My everlasting dominion, nor inhale the sweet savours of holiness breathing from My kingdom of sanctity.[11]

'What Will Other People Say?'

Am I always asking myself this question? Do I value the approval of others more than my own integrity? Conforming too closely to the opinions and customs of others may lead us to behaviour which in fact divides rather than unifies. For example, if I live in a neighbourhood where members of another race are looked down upon, do I always act with the conviction that all races are equal? Or am I subtly influenced to conceal my standards and behave as my neighbours do?

We need to act in a way which will make others feel that we are kind and friendly, and to that extent we should consider what other people will say. But in matters of principle we may have to ignore their opinions. They may think we are 'strange', but that is of no importance in comparison with our need to be just and loving towards all mankind.

In the Introduction to one of His books 'Abdu'l-

Bahá said of Himself:

> . . . for He, a wanderer in the desert of God's love,
> has come into a realm where the hand of denial or
> assent, of praise or blame, can touch Him not.[12]

Bahá'ís are not to strive to win praise, or to avoid
blame from their fellows. Praise is pleasant, and will
probably not spoil the person who, when praised,
remembers to thank God that he has been helped to
use his God-given abilities in a way that makes others
happy.

'I Must Get my Own Way'

The methods by which people try to dominate
others are of two types: the active, obvious methods,
and the less active, more indirect ones. Among the
active techniques are the use of physical force,
bullying, boasting, temper tantrums, and excessive
noisiness. Most of you who read this book will seldom
make use of these for getting your own way. It is in
the use of the less obvious methods that we often fail
to realize that the real purpose of our behaviour is to
compel another person to do what we want. We may
not approve of our own behaviour, while still not
understanding that it is an expression of self-love.

The following is a partial list of the questions we
should occasionally ask ourselves, in order to guard
against these methods of domination.

1. *Do I frequently find fault with others*, with
members of my family, friends, or those with whom I

work? Why am I so sure that my own way of feeling, thinking, and acting is so much better than theirs? Bahá'ís are left in no doubt as to the evils of fault-finding.

> O Son of Being! How couldst thou forget thine own faults and busy thyself with the faults of others? Whoso doeth this is accursed of Me.[13]

> O Emigrants! The tongue I have designed for the mention of Me, defile it not with detraction. If the fire of self overcome you, remember your own faults and not the faults of My creatures, inasmuch as every one of you knoweth his own self better than he knoweth others.[14]

> Beware lest ye offend the feelings of anyone, or sadden the heart of any person, or move the tongue in reproach of and finding fault with any-body, whether he is friend or stranger, believer or enemy.[15]

> Humanity is not perfect. There are imperfections in every human being and you will always become unhappy if you look toward the people themselves. But if you look toward God you will love them and be kind to them . . . Therefore do not look at the shortcomings of anybody; see with the sight of forgiveness. The imperfect eye beholds imperfections. The eye that covers faults looks toward the creator of souls.[16]

From the foregoing quotations it is clear that it is not only the *spoken* blame that we should avoid; we should not even *think* about the faults of others. The habit of resenting someone's behaviour in silence is so

insidious that it requires great self-discipline to overcome it.

If one wishes to stop fault-finding, the first requirement is to 'look toward God. . . toward the creator of
souls.' Then one should ask oneself, 'Why am I finding
fault? Is it to build up my own sense of importance,
my own feeling of virtue because I do not have this
particular shortcoming? Am I really accomplishing
anything constructive? If not, why waste my energy
on something which is destructive of unity and
friendliness?' Some people find it useful to learn by
heart two or three of the above quotations and, when
the thought of blaming another arises, to repeat the
quotation and meditate on its meaning. Thinking of
some of the praiseworthy qualities of the person who
has stirred us to fault-finding may put one in a more
positive frame of mind and heart.

The parent or teacher who has the responsibility of
educating children and youth must at times draw
attention to faults and errors, but this will have
comparatively little value unless it is done in a spirit
of friendliness. The use of reward and punishment in
the field of education will be discussed in a later
chapter.

2. *Do I engage in backbiting?* The dictionary
defines backbiting as 'speaking evil of the absent'.
Most of the quotations given under fault-finding
apply to backbiting. The seriousness of the latter is
emphasized in the following:

That seeker should, also, regard backbiting as grievous error, and keep himself aloof from its dominion, inasmuch as backbiting quencheth the light of the heart, and extinguisheth the life of the soul.[17]

3. *Do I listen to backbiting*, and by so doing encourage this characteristic in another person?

O Companion of My Throne! Hear no evil, and see no evil, abase not thyself, neither sigh nor weep. Speak no evil, that thou mayest not hear it spoken unto thee, and magnify not the faults of others that thine own faults may not appear great; and wish not the abasement of anyone, that thine own abasement be not exposed. . . .[18]

If John makes unkind remarks about Mary to me, what can I do? I can try to change the subject of conversation to something more constructive. I can counter with some of Mary's admirable traits, though sometimes this will stir up John to be still more critical. I may be able to leave John because I am needed elsewhere, or I may have to say, 'Mary is a friend of mine, and I really prefer not to hear her criticized. Let's talk about something else now.' If I can say this calmly, without annoyance or anger in my tone of voice, perhaps John will not be offended.

4. *Do I talk too much*, thereby depriving others of the opportunity to express their knowledge and ideas? Good conversation requires an *exchange* of experiences and ideas, and I have no right to assume

that what I wish to say is more important or more interesting than what other members of the group may have to contribute. Of course if, for example, I have attended an important conference, my friends will probably ask me to tell them about it, to give an informal 'lecture'; in which case a monologue is not 'talking too much'.

In a family of four or five members is there one person who does two-thirds of the talking? This is obviously unfair to the others; they may listen politely, but they probably do not enjoy hearing one voice so much of the time!

> For the tongue is a smouldering fire, and excess of speech a deadly poison. Material fire consumeth the body, whereas the fire of the tongue devoureth both heart and soul. The force of the former lasteth but for a time, whilst the effects of the latter endureth a century.[19]

5. *Do I talk too little*, depriving others of my ideas, experience, and knowledge? Am I afraid of making a mistake? Almost everyone will make mistakes when learning anything of real value: I must learn that 'a mistake is a friendly invitation to try again.' Besides, the idea I hesitate to give may be just what is needed by the group to push their thinking in a valuable direction.

6. *Do I speak with too loud a voice?* Often in a restaurant one voice rings out so loudly that people at nearby tables find it difficult to carry on a conver-

sation! And most children dislike a teacher who habitually yells at them. Of course, a person who is partially deaf may have difficulty adjusting the loudness of his voice to the needs of a situation, but the rest of us need not become a nuisance by speaking too loudly.

7. *Do I speak with too soft a voice*, so that others have to strain to hear what I am saying? When listeners lean forward in their seats, or even cup a hand behind an ear, I should realize that my voice is too low. A tone of voice which is habitually too low (just as much as one which is too loud) shows lack of consideration for others, and therefore indicates self-love.

8. *Am I argumentative and quarrelsome when presenting my ideas?* As will be seen later, in the chapter on Consultation, Bahá'ís are urged to avoid contentious discussion; they should *share* ideas, rather than carry on a debate.

> O Son of Dust! . . . Of all men the most negligent is he that disputeth idly and seeketh to advance himself over his brother. Say, O brethren! Let deeds, not words, be your adorning.[20]

9. *Do I use sarcasm,* hurting the feelings of others with my cutting remarks? Of all the verbal techniques for dominating people, sarcasm is probably the most cruel. It most surely sets a fire which 'devoureth both heart and soul'. Why be so unkind as to whip another with its stinging lash?

10. *Do I whine and complain?* Do I use tears as a method of getting my own way? If I do it is to tell others how sorry I am for myself, and that they must do something to make life easier for me. Whining and complaining are probably used as often by men as by women; they say to the listener, 'See how weak I am! You must take care of me, and see to it that I get what I want!' They indicate the 'clinging vine', who wishes to forgo responsibility for his own life. They show that the person is still using the behaviour of a badly-brought-up child. But now, in adulthood, we can learn to 'put away childish things'.

11. *Do I sulk?* Do I 'hold aloof in a sullenly ill-humoured or offended mood'? This is one of the meanest ways of trying to dominate another, because often the one thus attacked has no idea what he has done to displease. The intention is to make the other so miserable that he or she will never again dare to offend such an important person as the sulker.

To try to propitiate the one who sulks simply encourages him to use this technique again the next time he is offended. The best treatment is probably to ignore the sulking, and to pray that God will find a way to show the sulker the selfishness of his behaviour. (The person who maintains a sullen silence for three or four weeks is probably so neurotic that he needs professional treatment.)

12. *Do I give too much expression to my feelings of discouragement, depression, or sadness,* and thus

darken the lives of others? Certainly there are times
when a real sorrow needs to find expression, but this
is very different from habitual gloominess and pes-
simism. I should ask myself, 'Do I really wish to weigh
down others with my discouragement or sadness?
What is it that I am trying to get them to do for me?'

'Abdu'l-Bahá, who often greeted people by asking,
'Are you happy?', once wrote as follows to a man
who had suffered a great financial loss:

> Do not feel sorry; do not brood over the loss; do
> not sit down depressed; do not be silent; but, on
> the contrary, day and night be engaged in the com-
> memoration of the Lord in the greatest joy and
> gladness.[21]

13. *Am I habitually late for appointments?* If so,
I am really saying to the individual or group kept
waiting for me, 'Your time is less valuable than mine,
so it does not matter if I waste (steal) some of your
time. You should be willing to wait on my convenience.'

14. *Do I break my promises?* This, like habitual
lateness, shows lack of consideration for the feelings
and time of others. It is one way of being untruthful.
If I find that, because of circumstances beyond my
control, I am unable to keep a promise, I must
immediately let the other person know that I shall be
unable to do as I promised.

> Be worthy of the trust of thy neighbour, . . . a
> preserver of the sanctity of thy pledge. [22]

He should not wish for others that which he doth not wish for himself, nor promise that which he doth not fulful.[23]

15. *Am I frequently indecisive?* 'Do whichever you like; either way is all right with me.' 'I really have no preference. Which hat do *you* think I should buy?' And so on, time after time! My conscious intention may be to please the other person, but, when repeated again and again, such indecisiveness becomes a burden on the other. He would doubtless prefer me sometimes to have a 'mind of my own'.

16. *Do I make a boastful display* of my intelligence, my attainments, or my possessions? Do I 'show off'? If so, I make it clear that I wish to 'separate' myself from others.

If he is alloyed with the slightest trace of passion, desire, ostentation or self-interest, it is certain that the results of all efforts will prove fruitless, and he will become deprived and hopeless.[24]

17. *Do I show contempt for the feelings, ideas, or actions of others?* Such behaviour is more common than one might expect. 'Nice people' may not express contempt by saying, 'I think your idea is really stupid.' But this very same attitude can be conveyed by facial expression, tone of voice, or by completely ignoring the other's comment. Remarks such as, 'You are just being sentimental', or, 'I would not do that; it is poor taste', are often slightly veiled expressions of contempt. Standards of good and bad taste vary

from group to group, from culture to culture. Why should I assume that the standards of my group are superior to yours?

> Therefore no one should glorify himself over another; no one should manifest pride or superiority toward another; no one should look upon another with scorn and contempt . . .[25]

> '. . . it is in no wise permissible for one to belittle the thought of another . . .'[26]

18. *Do I demand special privileges,* so that others are deprived? Do I expect to have the most comfortable chair, the most honoured seat at the banquet, the highest office in the organization, the most devoted attention when I speak? Is it my intention that others shall be my servants?

Do I ever ask myself *why* I think I have a right to such special consideration?

19. *Do I dislike another person because he shows a character trait of my own, which I am trying to ignore in myself?* If I express an intense dislike for greediness, is it because I am really a greedy person? Certainly this is not true in every case, but I should be aware of the possibility, and be willing to do some honest 'soul searching'.

Psychologists are likely to say that the dominating techniques we have listed are aggressive responses to frustration, or expected frustration. This is true. But the Bahá'í must ask himself, 'If my purposes are frustrated and I respond by trying to dominate others, what kind of purposes are they? Are they the kind I wish to cherish? When I became a Bahá'í I committed my life to unity, love, and fellowship. In so far as I live in accord with these purposes I shall have no wish to dominate, and no need to respond to frustration with aggression.'

*   *   *

'O God, my God! Shield Thy trusted servants from the evils of self and passion, protect them with the watchful eye of Thy loving kindness from all rancour, hate and envy, shelter them in the impregnable stronghold of Thy Cause and, safe from the darts of doubtfulness, make them the manifestations of Thy glorious signs, illumine their faces with the effulgent rays shed from the Dayspring of Thy divine unity, gladden their hearts with the verses revealed from Thy holy kingdom, strengthen their loins by Thy all-swaying power that cometh from Thy Realm of Glory. Thou art the All-Bountiful, the Protector, the Almighty, the Gracious.'

'Abdu'l-Bahá

3

STRIVE FOR GENTLENESS AND LOVE

CHILDREN WHO ARE brought up in a home where out-going friendliness to everyone is the atmosphere of everyday living, are likely, almost unconsciously, to acquire the habit of responding in a friendly and loving way to others. But adults whose early lives were spent in homes where there was a great deal of unkindness may find, as they grow older, that they wish to become more loving. This is certainly true of many people who become Bahá'ís and then begin to realize how far their feelings and conduct fall below the Bahá'í standard of unity and love. This chapter will present some concrete suggestions as to how one may increase one's love and friendliness.

1. *Be gentle in your words and acts.* The Bahá'í Writings are overflowing with instructions concerning gentleness. The following are typical:

> We must associate with all humanity in gentleness and kindliness.[1]

> I hope that thou wilt progress more and more; . . . and that thou wilt ever strive for gentleness and love.[2]

> Therefore under no circumstances whatsoever should we assume any attitude except that of

gentleness and humility.[3]

Gentleness implies courtesy, forbearance, patience, and consideration. We live in a world which, in many of its aspects, is far from gentle. Therefore the adult who becomes a Bahá'í may find the acquisition of gentleness one of the most difficult ideals to attain.

Do not make the mistake of thinking that the gentle person has a weak character. Just the opposite is true: he has a character so strong that he does not need to shout at others, make unkind remarks, or do cruel things.

Remember that anger always interferes with understanding. It wastes time and energy, and produces no good result. Bahá'ís must use gentleness, not anger, in their contacts with others.

2. *Radiate joy to others.* Have you ever unexpectedly caught sight of a face in a mirror, and thought, 'Who is that glowering, unhappy creature?' and then, with shock, recognized your own face? Perhaps you were not unhappy, but merely deep in thoughtful concentration. However, others do not know this, and their day may be shadowed by your apparent darkness.

A person who possesses deep inner happiness and tranquillity actually remakes the contours and lines of his face, so that he cannot fail to be a joy-bringer to others. In one school in which I worked there was a woman in charge of the bookshop who radiated joy and good-will. If I passed her in the corridor and we merely exchanged 'good mornings', I felt the day had suddenly become brighter, and the world was a better place in which to live.

A Bahá'í was walking down the street, intent on serious business, when a boy of ten who had been watching him suddenly exclaimed, 'What makes you look so happy, Mister?'

Bahá'u'lláh has given each of us the responsibility of radiating joy to others.

> Be worthy of the trust of thy neighbour, and look upon him with a bright and friendly face.[4]

'Abdu'l-Bahá, in many letters and talks, made it clear that it is the love of God, reflected in the human face, which gives us the ability to brighten the lives of others.

> Let the love and light of the kingdom radiate through you until all who look upon you shall be illumined by its reflection.[5]

> All faces are dark except the face which is a mirror of the light of the love of divinity.[6]

> I pray for each and all that you may be as flames of love in the world, and that the brightness of your light and the warmth of your affection may reach the heart of every sad and sorrowing child of God.[7]

> May everyone point to you and ask 'Why are these people so happy?' I want you to be happy ... to laugh, smile and rejoice in order that others may be made happy by you.[8]

3. Be hospitable, to friends and strangers. Hospitality is of two kinds: planned occasions when guests are invited for tea or to spend the evening, and times when one or more people arrive *un*expectedly. They 'drop in' when they are driving past your home, or a neighbour 'runs over' just because she felt like talking to you.

One of the secrets of planned hospitality is to avoid making guests feel that you have made a tremendous effort on their behalf! If necessary, serve a very simple meal, in order to give friends the feeling that it has been easy for you to get ready for them, and you therefore can enjoy being with them. When you have week-end guests they should feel free to do what they want to do, although you will have some plans to suggest in case of need. One of the most satisfying compliments I have had on my own hospitality was the fact that a friend spent three hours on a Sunday afternoon utterly absorbed in a book to which I had drawn her attention.

There are women who are charming hostesses for planned hospitality, but are completely at a loss if unexpected guests arrive. An aunt of mine gave delightful teas and dinners. The food was delicious, the guests felt at ease, the conversation flowed naturally, the hostess was unflurried. But no one who knew her would have thought of just stopping by for a half-hour's chat.

It seems to me that true depth of hospitality is tested by the way one meets the unexpected guest.

The person who says, 'I hope you will come in any time you are in our neighbourhood', and really means it, shows that his friendliness works twenty-four hours a day. A Bahá'í pioneer to Africa told me, 'We never know how many people we are going to have for the next meal. Just before we start to prepare the food we count how many of those in the house will stay to eat.' This family did not have a large income, and they probably had to go without things they really needed for themselves in order to show such hospitality.

It is especially important for children and teenagers to feel free to bring their friends home. After an afternoon of hard play the ten-year-old boy who can say to another boy, 'Let's go to my house and make some cocoa', is showing friendliness in a way the other understands and appreciates. If the cost of such entertainment must be considered, the mother may say to her son, 'There is this much cocoa and this box of cookies which you may use after school this week, so plan your invitations accordingly.'

The recipients of 'unplanned hospitality' have a responsibility to be considerate of the *time* of host and hostess. If your casual call lasts for three hours you have probably kept your hostess from too much of the work she needed to do that day. If you find that your friends are entertaining invited guests perhaps it would be better to stay fifteen minutes and then leave.

The standard of Bahá'í hospitality is stated in a

talk on marriage attributed to 'Abdu'l-Bahá (quoted in full in chapter 10).

> Make your home a haven of rest and peace. Be hospitable, and let the doors of your house be open to the faces of friends and strangers. Welcome every guest with radiant grace and let each feel that it is his own home.[9]

4. *Give special attention to befriending strangers.*

> Be kind to the strangers . . .
> Help to make them feel at home; find out where they are staying, ask if you may render them any service; try to make their lives a little happier.[10]

> . . . deal with the strangers as you deal with the friends, be ye gentle toward the outsiders as you are toward the beloved ones . . .[11]

> Do ye not see foreignness, nay rather, know all as friends; for with the observation of strangeness, the practice of love and unity is difficult.[12]

I was once travelling alone through a country with which the United States had no diplomatic relations. I had problems with regard to customs, exit permit, etc., which seemed insoluble. Then an English business man, who knew the language of the country and the complicated official procedures, came to my assistance, and within a few days I was out of the country, with all my baggage intact. I learned then how much strangers may need to be befriended, and how grateful one is for such kindly help.

5. *Visit those who are ill.* If a person is sick for a
long time, he probably needs your visits more after
weeks of illness than he did at the beginning.

> We should all visit the sick. When they are in
> sorrow and suffering it is a real help and benefit to
> have a friend come. Happiness is a great healer to
> those who are ill. . . . The people in the east show
> the utmost kindness and compassion to the sick
> and suffering. This has greater effect than the
> remedy itself. You must always have this thought
> of love and affection when you visit the ailing and
> afflicted.[13]

6. *Develop skill in finding the 'real person'* behind
an awkward or unfriendly face. If such a person is assured of your kindly understanding he will, eventually, dare to let you see his real self. In order to
develop this skill, one must forget oneself so completely that one sees the world through the eyes of
the other. Ask yourself, 'Why is he afraid to be
friendly? Has he been hurt too often by the unkindness of others? Is he fearful of saying the wrong thing?'

Approach such a person by trusting his good intentions, as you wish him to trust yours. If he is hesitant
in accepting your friendly advances he may be
thinking, 'I wonder if he will like me. Is he thinking
I am stupid and uninteresting? Perhaps my clothes are
out of place. I wish I were more sure of myself!' If
you are lovingly accepting this person as he is, in time
he will trust you and come half way to meet your
friendliness.

7. *Find out the interests of the other person.* Relate them to your own if possible. Be a good listener to information and ideas which are not familiar to you. But do not ask too many questions, especially about aspects of the other's personal life which he may consider none of your business.

8. *Try to adapt to the conventions of others* when you talk to them. Customs differ greatly from country to country, and from group to group. Actions which to me show good manners may seem impolite to one who has been brought up in a different society. As a child I was taught that it was bad manners to ask a person I did not know well, 'How much did you *pay* for that?' But in Africa I find that many truly courteous people ask this question, with no thought of being impolite.

At the Green Acre school, which many of us attended summer after summer, we called one another by our first names. A very dignified elderly gentleman, a new Bahá'í, began to come to the school, and everyone called him *Mr.* Martin. One day I asked him if he would like to be called by his first name. He answered, 'Yes, I would. When you all call me *Mr.* Martin it makes me feel shut out of the group.' On the other hand, a friend who was involved in Bahá'í teaching on one of the islands of the West Indies told me that all the Bahá'ís there expected to be called Miss, Mr., or Mrs. They felt that they were not *respected* if they were called by their first names.

Many of these customs are morally neither right nor wrong. They are just what people are used to, and the friendly Bahá'í should make an effort not to shock people by acting contrary to their customs.

9. *Give advice only when asked,* and then only by gentle, tactful suggestion. Never blame another, in the slightest degree, if he does not take your advice. Too often we are *certain* that we know what is for the other's good, and we persist in trying to get him to accept our ideas. Perhaps what we suggest is the best possible thing for him to do, but it may not be, and every adult should have the right to make his own mistakes!

10. *Use imagination to protect another from 'losing face'.* No one likes to be made to feel inferior, or that he is under heavy obligation to another. If you tell a friend how far you have driven out of your way, in order to take him to a meeting, he is likely to wish that he had stayed at home. If you give a gift, the recipient should feel the pleasure you had in selecting it, rather than how grateful he should be.

You will probably not intentionally do anything to make a friend 'lose face', but you may see a third person do something to humiliate another. In such a case, you can often do or say something to take the sting out of the humiliation. If Anne tells Jane that her refreshments at the last Bahá'í gathering were much too elaborate, perhaps you can say, 'Oh, but I think once in a while it is a good idea to have something really special!' Or, to take a more serious example, Thomas said to John, 'Your son, Paul, has such badly bent legs that he looks like a dwarf. It is too bad you have such a cripple!' Thomas's wife, who was listening, said, 'Perhaps Paul began to walk before his legs were strong enough. But he is only three years old, and his legs can be straightened if his mother and John will have him do every day some exercises that I will show them. It may take a long time, but it can be done. He certainly isn't a cripple!'

By quick thinking and by entering imaginatively into the life of another, you can often save him from unhappiness and humiliation.

11. *Be generous in giving praise when you can do so honestly.* But do not flatter. Exaggerated praise may please for the moment, but later the one who received it will realize that it was undeserved, and will distrust your future compliments.

Use wisdom in choosing the time and place for giving praise. This is especially important in the case of teenagers, who are often embarrassed when praised in the presence of older people.

12. *If another expresses appreciation of what you have done, accept it graciously.* Avoid false modesty. When a friend praises an action of yours, you imply a criticism of his judgement if you say, 'I thought it was quite bad.' How much more pleasant and courteous to say, 'I am very glad you liked it.'

13. *Give your acquaintance or your friend an opportunity to help you.* Even when you feel that it might be easier to do the piece of work yourself, his offering to help means that he wishes to make a contribution to your life. It is kind to permit or even invite him to do so. Many people are reassured by the feeling that someone they do not know very well wants and likes to work with them.

14. *Encourage a group of friends to work together towards a goal which you all value.* If the aim towards which a group works is one which all the members really value, then small differences and personality conflicts will tend to disappear and the success will be greater than any one individual could have achieved alone. Bahá'ís are motivated by deep devotion to divinely-inspired purposes, and this makes it possible for people of the most diverse abilities and backgrounds to work together effectively.

15. *Be responsible when you make a promise.* Think carefully; never promise something unless you believe you can carry it out. Why should someone believe what you tell him about Bahá'u'lláh if you have shown yourself untrustworthy in everyday affairs?

16. *Frequently remind yourself of the 'miracles' that love achieves.*

Love is the one means that insures true felicity both in this world and the next. Love is the light that guideth in darkness, the living link that uniteth God with man, that assureth the progress of every illumined soul. Love is the most great Law that ruleth this mighty and heavenly cycle . . . Love is the spirit of life unto the adorned body of mankind . . .[14]

Love gives life to the lifeless. Love lights a flame in the heart that is cold. Love brings hope to the hopeless and gladdens the hearts of the sorrowful.
In the world of existence there is indeed no greater power than the power of love.[15]

Until loves takes possession of the heart no other divine bounty can be revealed in it.[16]

Perhaps you are thinking, 'I would like to be loving and friendly and follow all these suggestions, but it is just too difficult! Where can I get the *will* to break old habits and form so many new ones?'

The Bahá'í teachings give a clear answer to this question. Unselfish love for others is a reflection of our love for God. As a man's love for God increases, his love for other human beings is bound to increase. He can, by taking thought, improve his methods of expressing that love, but the basic requirement is so to love God that one reflects the light of that love on others.

Meditate on the following quotations which state simply and clearly the relation of the love of God to the love of people.

Real love is impossible unless one turn his face towards God and be attracted to His Beauty.[17]

The love of the human world has shone forth from the love of God, and has appeared by the bounty and grace of God.

. . . this greatest power in the human world is the love of God. It brings the different peoples under the shadow of the tent of affection. . .[18]

. . . all humanity must be looked upon with love, kindness and respect, for what we behold in them are none other than the signs and traces of God himself.[19]

When you love a member of your family or a compatriot, let it be with a ray of the Infinite Love! Let it be in God, and for God! Wherever you find the attributes of God love that person, whether he be of your family or of another. Shed the light of a boundless love on every human being whom you meet . . .

. . . *All* Humanity! Every human being! *never forget this!*[20]

The great unselfish love for humanity . . . is the one perfect love, possible to all mankind, and can only be achieved by the power of the Divine Spirit.[21]

Lay aside all self-purposes and know for a certainty that all men are the servants of one God who will bind them together in love and agreement.[22]

4

ACTION AND ACHIEVEMENT

EVERY HUMAN BEING needs to feel that he is of some value, of some worth to the world. It is right for us to feel this, for we are created by God, and therefore have the capacity to grow into valuable people. To feel oneself 'no good', a nonentity, is acute misery. It makes a person think, 'Since I am nothing, of no worth to anyone, I should never have been born.'

If he dwells upon the thought of non-existence he will become utterly incompetent; with weakened will-power his ambition for progress will be lessened and the acquisition of human virtues will cease.[1]

We should distinguish between feeling of value and feeling superior. The latter implies that I feel myself 'better than others', that I wish to be able to look down on them. Usually the man with a strong feeling of superiority makes very little contribution to mankind, he deludes himself with imaginary achievements, or he is actively destructive.

We may also note the difference between the *fact* of inferiority and the *feeling* of inferiority. All of us are inferior in many things which we cannot do well. An objective recognition of such lack of achievement is one indication of maturity. It is only when we give too much time and energy to comparing ourselves with others that we are in danger of developing feelings of inferiority.

How many of our daily problems arise from false ideas of what makes a life valuable! Is Mary's idea of a friend that of a person who always does what she wishes? Is John's standard of success in business that of giving as little as possible in return for what he receives? Does Carol measure the value of her life by the number of boy-friends she takes away from other girls?

The best basis for feeling that one is a valuable human being is contribution to the life of one's fellow men. This means constructive, creative, co-operative *action.* Each of us should ask ourselves, 'How much of my energy am I using constructively? How much destructively? How much of it is spent in trivialities which have no meaning?'

> The essence of faith is fewness of words and abundance of deeds; he whose words exceed his deeds, know verily his death is better than his life.[2]

> ... all effort and exertion put forth by man from the fullness of his heart is worship, if it is prompted by the highest motives and the will to do service to humanity.[3]

> The wrong in the world continues to exist just because people talk only of their ideals, and do not strive to put them into practice. . . .
> A man who does great good, and talks not of it, is on the way to perfection.[4]

Too Little Action

Why is it that some people take too little action to meet the needs of their daily lives? The first reason that should always be considered is low physical vitality, due to some malfunctioning of the body. The remedy is, obviously, treatment by a competent doctor.

A second reason is that too many people spend their energy in a search for 'magic', rather than in constructive activity. They imagine that they can 'get something for nothing' without effort on their part. Newspapers and magazines are filled with magic promises of easy roads to achievement, or the word 'new' is used as a magic 'come on' to convince the reader that a miracle of manufacturing has been achieved. Of course we wish to have improvements made in the products we use, but we should make sure that there is real improvement, and not be misled by 'magic words'.

A different form of magic which often reduces activity is day-dreaming. How easy, how pleasant, how satisfying to my ego, are the heights I gain in my day-dreams! And while I indulge in these visionary fancies, who is doing the work I am neglecting? Of course, the imaginative planning of work which is later carried out should not be confused with day-dreaming.

Inactivity is sometimes the result of fear and discouragement. If one's honest efforts have been met time after time with criticism, harshness, or neglect, one may decide that it is better to be inactive. If parents continually blame or even punish a child who has done his very best at a task, perhaps his increasing inactivity is a sign of intelligence. Discouraged children seldom become contributing, creative adults.

Finally, lack of adequate activity may be due to absence of strong purposes and ideals. The early life of an individual may not have given him opportunities for developing lively interests. Poverty, illness, too restricted an environment, the fears of his parents, all may account for the weakness of his interests, and therefore of his purposes. A young man of twenty-five who was being treated by a psychologist said he could not think of *anything* in which he was interested. It was only after several weeks of treatment that he said vaguely that drama might interest him a little. It was through participation in a drama club that he finally came back into contact with active life.

> For an unlit candle, however great in diameter and tall, is no better than a barren palm tree or a pile of dead wood.[5]

> If haste is harmful, inertness and indolence are a thousand times worse.[6]

Misdirected Activity

You may know a person whose days are filled with activity, but who seems to achieve little. His actions are misdirected. Perhaps his purpose is not defined clearly enough, or he may vacillate from one purpose to another. This may occur when his stated purpose and his real inner desire are in conflict. For example, he says he is a friend of John's, and he thinks he *should* be, but actually he would be pleased if 'that conceited fellow' were humiliated.

Misdirected action is frequently the result of a lack of knowledge and experience. If one realizes this, the lack can be corrected through an effort to increase knowledge, and through an objective analysis of one's experiences. Failure to use one's intelligence also results in ineffective action. (See chapter 5).

Undertaking too many activities is a common form of misdirected action. Colloquially we speak of the person who is 'trying to run in all directions at once'. Such hyperactivity sometimes has a physical cause in some glandular disturbance. It may also be due to an excess of ambition, or to a mistaken sense of duty which causes one to agree to do all the things one is asked to do.

Selection among activities is essential, and we should select in terms of what we value most. 'Abdu'l-Bahá once wrote:

> When the 'Most Important' work is before our sight, we must let go the 'Important' one.[7]

From their early years children should have experience in choosing which activity they wish to undertake, and then they should be expected to carry their choice through to completion. Two young brothers had their birthdays within a few days of each other, and usually they had a combined party to which they invited their friends. When their eighth and tenth birthdays were approaching, each boy was eager to be given a watch which cost about ten dollars. Their mother said to them, 'If we buy you the watches we cannot afford to give you a party. Which will you choose?' Experiences of this type will help develop adults who will make intelligent selections among activities, and who will not waste their energy in dashing from one thing to another.

Have you met the hard worker who frequently exclaims, 'I just have *so* much to do! I don't see how I will *ever* get it done!' This seems to relieve the feelings of the speaker, but eventually the listener gets tired of vicariously taking on the burdens of the other. If the speaker is the mother of five children and does all the cooking and housework, is also lovingly training the children, and not neglecting her husband, one should listen sympathetically to her weary complaints of 'too much to do'. But the complainer who has 'so much work' because of failure to select among activities which are not his responsibility should not tire or bore others by telling them how overworked he is!

Bahá'ís are often asked to undertake more work than they have time and energy to do well. They have to select in terms of the 'most important', and other Bahá'ís should not criticize them for their refusal to take on everything.

The Characteristics of Balanced Activity

The mature person whose action is useful to his fellows has clearly-defined purposes. He makes careful, long-range plans for accomplishing each one. If he does not have the knowledge needed, he does not proceed until he has acquired it. When he is ready to act, he goes ahead with assurance, economy of motion, and inner tranquillity. Those who observe him say, 'He does it so *easily*!'

The truly religious person will, throughout his planning and action, ask for the guidance of the Divine Spirit; but he does not expect God to do all the work! He uses the abilities God has given him, and trusts that He will help him not to make serious mistakes.

> When you call on the Mercy of God waiting to reinforce you, your strength will be tenfold.[8]

The mature individual respects the 'pace' of others. He does not become impatient with the person who is, temperamentally, a slow-mover. He tries not to be disturbed by the extreme speed with which some others act. When people are carrying out a group activity, differences in pace may be a source of disturbance unless each one shows consideration for the varying speeds with which others think and act.

The moderation and inner calm of balanced activity is conducive to good health. All of us at times have to act under great outer pressures, but if we can keep our spirits tranquil we are not likely to develop ulcers or other psychosomatic illnesses.

When the mature individual has completed an activity he evaluates the results. Which were thoroughly satisfactory? Which could be improved? If most of the results were unsatisfactory, then were the mistakes made in defining the goal, in drawing up the plans, or in putting the plans into effect?

> The attainment of any object is conditioned upon knowledge, volition and action. Unless these three conditions are forthcoming there is no execution or accomplishment.[9]

> ... every great Cause in this world of existence findeth a visible expression through three means; first, intention; second, confirmation; third, action. ... For the intention, the power and the action, all the three essential elements are brought together and the realization of everything in the contingent world dependeth upon these three principles.[10]

Through the kind of action we have called 'balanced' a person develops a sense of true personal worth; he feels that he is a channel for the Divine Purpose to use.

> Let your actions cry aloud to the world that you are indeed Bahá'ís, for it is *actions* that speak to the world and are the cause of the progress of humanity. . . .
> . . . It is not through lip-service only that the elect of God have attained to holiness, but by patient lives of active service they have brought light into the world.[11]

Steps in Habit Formation

Much of our everyday action is based on habit. In our daily work, habits save time and energy. Our friendliness towards others can become habitual; we say, 'It is only *natural* for me to act like that', but actually we have *learned* how to act so that we make others happy to be with us.

Often we find that we do not like some of our old habits and we wish to form new ones. This is sometimes very difficult, and the following steps in habit formation may be helpful.

1. First, ask yourself, 'Do I really want to change? Is my desire great enough to keep me working at it? Do I truly believe that it is possible for me to change?'

... in the choice of good and bad actions [man] is free, and he commits them according to his own will.[12]

2. When you decide to form a new habit, you must start with real determination to succeed.

Success or failure, gain or loss, must ... depend upon man's own exertions. The more he striveth, the greater will be his progress.[13]

Endeavour, ceaseless endeavour, is required. Nothing short of an indomitable determination can possibly achieve it.[14]

3. Do not allow any exceptions to occur until the new habit is well established. If, in order to lose weight, you decide not to eat anything between meals,

do not think up good reasons why you need an occasional midnight lunch!

> Everything of importance in this world demands the close attention of its seeker. The one in pursuit of anything must undergo difficulties and hardships until the object in view is attained and the great success is obtained.[15]

> ... without firmness and steadfastness no matter shall prove effective in existence.[16]

4. *Make* opportunities for practising the habit, rather than avoiding situations that call for its practice.

> All that which ye potentially possess can, however, be manifested only as a result of your own volition.[17]

5. Often two or three close friends can help one another. In breaking some habits the most difficult factor is becoming conscious of what one is doing. For example, whenever Sally was greatly interested in something her voice became very high and shrill. Even when her friend Grace drew this to her attention, Sally often did not notice how shrill her voice was. After talking this over, the two girls agreed that whenever Sally's voice rose, Grace would say softly, 'Voice down.' If this were in a group, where this comment might embarrass Sally, Grace raised her hand and brought it down slowly, to serve as a reminder. After a few weeks of such help Sally learned to keep her voice pleasantly low.

An intimate group of six Bahá'ís met once a week to study some of the Writings on character development. Each week they read about some character trait that all of them wished to acquire. During the following week each one tried to practise it. When they met again they exchanged experiences, discussed the problems they had encountered, and encouraged one another to persevere. From these readings and discussions the friends felt that their habits had shown definite improvement.

6. Do not try to make too many habit changes at once! The danger in doing so is that you may make little improvement in any of them, and so will become discouraged and give up all efforts to change. Choose two or three habits to work on, and when you feel that you have achieved reasonable success, begin to work on two or three others.

7. Sometimes it is helpful to make a written record of progress. This is especially useful with children.

8. Throughout the period of forming a habit, pray for strength to persevere. Let prayer remind you of the reasons for forming the habit.

Therefore strive that your actions day by day may be beautiful prayers. Turn towards God, and seek always to do that which is right and noble.[18]

5

THE USE OF INTELLIGENCE

REFERENCES TO HUMAN intelligence and its importance are woven, like a shining thread, throughout the Bahá'í Writings. The concept of intelligence is variously worded: intellect, reason, mind, understanding, rational soul. As will be seen in the quotations which follow, shades of difference among these words are sometimes implied, but the basic meaning is the same.

Man's Intelligence is God-Given

Man's intelligence is a gift from God; it is a *spiritual* reality.

> It is the light of the *intellect* which gives us knowledge and understanding . . .
> This light of the intellect is the highest light that exists, for it is born of the *Light Divine.* [1]

> All blessings are divine in origin but none can be compared with this power of intellectual investigation and research which is an eternal gift producing fruits of unending delight. [2]

> If we insist that such and such a subject is not to be reasoned out and tested according to the established logical modes of the intellect, what is the use of the reason which God has given man? [3]

However great the importance of human intelligence, it gives only a faint indication of the Mind of God. While men should use their intellects to their fullest capacity, it should be with a realization of the Source of their abilities.

No matter how far the human intelligence may advance, it is still but a drop while divine omniscience is the ocean.[4]

Purposes for which Intelligence Should Be Used

The use of one's intelligence should be a source of satisfaction and joy. But delight in thinking is not the main purpose for which God gave intellect to mankind.

First and foremost among these favours, which the Almighty hath conferred upon man, is the gift of understanding. . . . This gift giveth man the power to discern the truth in all things, leadeth him to that which is right, and helpeth him to discover the secrets of creation.[5]

God's greatest gift to man is that of intellect, or understanding. . . .
God gave this power to man that it might be used for the advancement of civilization, for the good of humanity, to increase love and concord and peace.[6]

The power of the rational soul can discover the realities of things . . . and penetrate the mysteries of existence. All sciences, knowledge, arts, wonders, institutions, discoveries, and enterprises come from the exercised intelligence of the rational soul.[7]

To fail to use our intelligence, to make no effort to improve in our use of this gift, is irresponsible, as well as extremely wasteful. (Remember Christ's parable of the talents!)

> God has endowed man with intelligence and reason whereby he is required to determine the verity of questions and propositions.[8]

Since intelligence is an aspect of man's spirit, it is immortal. Its use is not confined to this earth-life, and we may assume that in the timelessness of eternity our minds will serve purposes of which we now have not the faintest hint.

> The intelligence of man, his reasoning powers, his knowledge, his scientific achievements, all these being manifestations of the spirit, partake of the inevitable law of spiritual progress and are, therefore, of necessity, immortal.[9]

Independent Investigation

One of the basic principles which Bahá'u'lláh gave to the world is that each individual must investigate truth for himself. He should not be enchained by inherited beliefs, by superstitions, by prejudices, by propaganda. We must be free to use our intelligence justly.

This principle does not mean that we should refuse to accept the results of careful scientific research. 'Abdu'l-Bahá illustrated this by saying that the skill of a doctor must first be ascertained, and then the patient should do what the physician tells him to, whether he likes it or not!

Too many people have not been taught how to recognize sound research and investigation. If a scientist presents conclusions which they do not like, they refuse to accept them. Or, on the other hand, they agree uncritically with the pronouncements of a 'big name'.

> What does it mean to investigate reality? It means that man must forget all hearsay and examine truth himself; for he does not know whether statements he hears are in accordance with reality or not.[10]

> If five people meet together to seek for truth, they must begin by cutting themselves free from all their own special conditions and renouncing all preconceived ideas. . . .

> It means, also, that we must be willing to clear away all that we have previously learned, all that would clog our steps on the way to truth; we must not shrink if necessary from beginning our education all over again.[11]

> The investigating mind is attentive, alive; the mind callous and indifferent is deaf and dead.[12]

One of the areas in which independent investigation is of the greatest importance is that of religion. The Bahá'í Faith insists that religion and science must be in harmony, and that both must be reasonable.

> If we say religion is opposed to science we either lack knowledge of true science or true re-

ligion, for both are founded upon the premises and conclusions of reason and both must bear its test.[13]

Shall man gifted with the power of reason unthinkingly follow and adhere to dogma, creeds and hereditary beliefs which will not bear the analysis of reason in this century of effulgent reality?[14]

How can man believe that which he knows to be opposed to reason? Is this possible? Can the heart accept that which reason denies? Reason is the first faculty of man and the religion of God is in harmony with it.[15]

If religion were contrary to logical reason then it would cease to be a religion and be merely a tradition. Religion and science are the two wings upon which man's intelligence can soar into the heights, with which the human soul can progress.[16]

Bahá'ís are sometimes asked, 'How do you reconcile the use of your intelligence with your acceptance of the idea that the Prophet, or Manifestation of God, has perfect wisdom and that you must obey His commands and follow His suggestions?'

Before a person becomes a Bahá'í he has become convinced that Bahá'u'lláh is the spiritual *expert* for this age, that He has perfect knowledge of spiritual law. He arrives at this by study of the life of Bahá'u'lláh by learning how the lives of those who have accepted His teachings have been changed, by reading His creative Writings, and, finally, by an inner assurance that no other power can heal the ills of the world. He has

used his intelligence to investigate the claims of the
Faith, and has become convinced of Bahá'u'lláh's
own statement:

> That which the Lord hath ordained as the
> sovereign remedy and mightiest instrument for the
> healing of all the world is the union of all its
> peoples in one universal Cause, one common Faith.
> This can in no wise be achieved except through the
> power of a skilled, an all-powerful and inspired
> Physician.[17]

'Abdu'l-Bahá states the comparison with the knowledge and skill of the physician in these words:

> In the same way, the skilled doctor in treating
> the patient 'does what he wishes', and the patient
> has no right to object; whatever the doctor says
> and does is right; all ought to consider him the
> manifestation of these words, 'He does what he
> wishes, and commands whatever he desires'. . . . The
> skill of the doctor must be first ascertained; but
> when the skill of the doctor is once established, 'he
> does what he wishes'.[18]

When a man has accepted Bahá'u'lláh as his
'Physician' he finds that his need to use his intelligence has really just begun. How can he best *apply*
these teachings in everyday living? How can he apply
them in making the greatest contribution to mankind
of which he is capable? The true Bahá'í never reaches
the day when he is free to abandon the use of intelligence and love.

Some Errors in the Use of Intelligence

One way to improve in the use of one's intelligence is to know some of the common errors and thus be able consciously to guard against them.

1. *Failure to define the problem accurately.* Do you confuse the following: 'Ought I?' 'Do I wish to?' 'Is it feasible?' For example, 'Do I think I ought to leave my home country to go as a Bahá'í teacher to the Canary Islands?' 'Is that the place I *wish* to go, or do I really want to go to Peru? Or would I actually prefer to stay at home?' 'Since I have high blood pressure, is it wise to go to a place with a high altitude?' I should answer each of these questions as honestly as I can, and my thinking will probably be more accurate because I have dealt with the three aspects separately, rather than trying to answer the one question, 'Where shall I go as a Bahá'í teacher?'

2. *Incomplete analysis* of the probable results of a course of action. (See the section below on the use of intelligence in making choices.)

3. *Generalizing from too few cases.* For example, I know two elderly people whose feelings are easily hurt and I conclude, 'Unfortunately as people grow older they become very sensitive to any supposed slight.' Or, I have met three Persian Bahá'ís who seem to have little understanding of Bahá'í administration, and I say, 'Isn't it strange that the Persians do not learn how to consult in Assembly meetings and committees?'

4. *Lack of adequate facts* and, often, failure to recognize that lack. How much of my information about the current world scene comes from prejudiced newspapers and magazines? To take another example, Martha thought she heard Betty making an uncomplimentary remark about her reading aloud; it was not till weeks later that Martha learned that Betty had been talking about her cousin Marcia.

5. *Lack of imagination in thinking of possible solutions to a problem.* Here a group working together can usually think of more good possibilities than can the most intelligent person when working alone. Thinking of possible solutions frequently requires patience; it cannot be done in a hurry. One must often be willing to 'mull over' the problem for days or weeks, trusting that one idea will be the seed from which others will grow.

Rúḥíyyih Khánum said she considered that three of Shoghi Effendi's outstanding traits were audacity, ingenuity, and economy. An interesting illustration of his combining the second and third of these, was his solution to the problem of finding an inexpensive material for covering the paths around the Shrine of the Báb on Mount Carmel. His answer was to get broken red roof-tiles from places where old houses had been demolished. These were put into a machine which crushed them to small bits, which then made an attractive and economical covering for the many paths.

6. *Inflexibility of attitudes and ideas* is one of the

most common errors in the use of intelligence, and is probably one of the most difficult to correct. The person who gives as a reason for his behaviour, 'I have *always* done it this way', may be ignoring present facts which make a change desirable. The inflexible individual depends on the familiar for his security; he may have a deep fear of any change in his habitual responses. By his refusal to experiment with new foods, new ways of travel, new methods of group action, he misses valuable and interesting experiences. Does he realize that narrow experience results in limited thinking?

In the field of religion, dependence on *ritual* may cause a person to fail to experience real depth of spiritual insight. Flexibility in worship keeps the mind and spirit 'attentive, alive'.

We should each ask ourselves, 'Do I have some out-moded habits which are useless or even harmful? If so, why do I keep them? Do I want to stay in these deadening ruts?' Are there words or phrases to which you react with more emotion than is really justified? These may be danger signals which indicate areas of inflexibility.

I do not, of course, mean to suggest that all change is desirable. It is the unwillingness to give a fair, objective consideration to new ideas and methods of action that is a handicap in the use of intelligence. Young children who are secure in the love of their parents welcome new experiences, a different kind of toy, a story about strange people and customs, a trip to a place they have not been before. What has gone wrong in the early life of the inflexible adult?

In becoming a Bahá'í a person opens his life to a flood of new experiences. He must not hesitate to 'begin his education all over again'. The extent of the changes he must accept gladly are suggested in the following statement of Bahá'u'lláh.

> The world's equilibrium hath been upset through the vibrating influence of this most great, this new World Order. Mankind's ordered life hath been revolutionized through the agency of this unique, this wondrous System — the like of which mortal eyes have never witnessed.[19]

The Use of Intelligence in Making Choices

Some of the choices which we make have little practical or ethical significance. These are matters of personal preference. Shall I wear the blue or the pink dress? Which of these three pictures shall I hang in the dining-room? Shall I plant tulips or daffodils in this border?

Occasionally an emergency requires a very quick decision; we would prefer to consider the choice with care, but there is no time. If there is a fire in the kitchen of my house and I think I have five minutes to remove things from the living-room, shall I take out furniture or books or papers? Or perhaps I hear a plane very close, and it sounds as though it has bad engine trouble, which might bring it to earth any minute. Will my children be safer inside or outside the house? My responses in such emergencies will be the result of many past choices, and of my emotional stability.

The choices for which we should consciously use our intelligence are practical, or ethical, or frequently a combination of the two. For example — (1) Edith must decide whether to go to X or Y college, at both of which she has been accepted. (2) Stephen has an offer of a well-paid position in California, but all his family and friends live in Maine, where he now has a fairly good salary. Shall he go to California? (3) Philip has in view a summer job with good pay for a young man of twenty years of age. He has also been invited to be a sports teacher in a Bahá'í Summer School, with maintenance but no salary. He must choose between the two.

The following procedure should help you in making a wise choice between two courses of action. Analyse as carefully as possible both the advantages and disadvantages of each course, and list these *in writing*. (The written list tends to increase accuracy and completeness, and helps you to remember important factors.) If you need more information do not fail to get it. Your *interest*, or lack of interest, should be included as one factor. After you have made the lists as complete as you can, ask one or more close friends to suggest aspects you may have omitted.

The procedure will probably be made clearer by an example. Charles Gray, thirty-five years old, has been working in a research job with a large company for the past ten years. He has thought vaguely that 'sometime he must make a change' to work that makes better use of his training and ability, but he has done nothing about it. Suddenly, with no fore-warning, he is offered a research job in a city a thousand miles away from his home. He goes for an interview, and his wife goes with him, to try to find out what conditions of living would be if they moved. They return home, with the agreement that Charles will definitely accept or reject the position at the end of a month.

Charles realizes that such a change is a very important one, not only for himself, but also for his wife and their two children. He begins to analyse the reasons for and against taking the new job, and only then begins to appreciate how many factors in his present position are not satisfactory. After much discussion with his wife and two close friends he draws up a table of advantages and disadvantages, to help him in making his decision.

It is clear that the new position would give Charles much more satisfaction in his actual work; but his present job is better for salary, tenure, and pension. He realizes that the kind of service he could give the Bahá'í Faith in the new city would require more real effort and initiative, and he wonders if he could live up to that challenge.

Charles and his wife are then face to face with the question, 'What do we value most?' An honest answer to it is an essential part of their making an *intelligent* choice.

In the same way, you, when confronted with two courses of action, must decide what you value most. It may be that one factor 'weighs' more heavily than all the others, thus leading to your decision. It is important to be fully conscious of the values which determine the final choice; this may protect you against much disappointment in the future.

After you have used your intelligence and knowledge to their fullest, pray that God will help you make a decision which is in accord with His purposes. Then act, with assurance and confidence.

*   *   *

'O God, refresh and gladden my spirit. Purify my heart. Illumine my mind. I lay all my affairs in Thy hand. Thou art my Guide and my Refuge. I will no longer be sorrowful and grieved; I will be a happy and joyful being. O God! I will no longer be full of anxiety, nor will I let trouble harass me. I will not dwell on the unpleasant things of life. O God! Thou art kinder to me than I am to myself. I dedicate myself to Thee, O Lord.'

'Abdu'l-Bahá

6

THE USE OF MONEY

THE WAY IN which an individual makes use of money and possessions is an important indication of his psychological and spiritual maturity. His first responsibility is to earn a livelihood. The able-bodied, mentally sound man, who has an opportunity to work but does not do so, and expects others to support him, shows a marked degree of immaturity. The Bahá'í teachings about earning a living are clearly stated by Bahá'u'lláh:

> It is enjoined upon every one of you to engage in some form of occupation, such as crafts, trades and the like. We have graciously exalted your engagement in such work to the rank of worship unto God, the True One.... Waste not your time in idleness and sloth. Occupy yourselves with that which profiteth yourselves and others....
> The most despised of men in the sight of God are those who sit idly and beg.[1]

> O My Servants! Ye are the trees of My garden; ye must give forth goodly and wondrous fruits, that ye yourselves and others may profit therefrom. Thus it is incumbent on every one to engage in crafts and professions, for therein lies the secret of wealth, O men of understanding! For results depend upon means, and the grace of God shall be all-sufficient unto you. Trees that yield no fruit have been and will ever be for the fire.[2]

O My Servant! The best of men are they that earn a livelihood by their calling and spend upon themselves and upon their kindred for the love of God, the Lord of all worlds.[3]

Should a man wish to adorn himself with the ornaments of the earth, to wear its apparels, or partake of the benefits it can bestow, no harm can befall him, if he alloweth nothing whatever to intervene between him and God, for God hath ordained every good thing ... for such of His servants as truly believe in Him. Eat ye, O people, of the good things which God hath allowed you, and deprive not yourselves from His wondrous bounties.[4]

The third and fourth of these quotations are of special interest here because of the connection made between spending and the love of God. All the things of use and beauty which man can make from the materials God has provided are for his enjoyment, provided that they do not separate him from God. This proviso places on each individual the responsibility of deciding whether a given purchase might decrease his nearness to God. The regular, necessary expenditures of every day fall into a pattern, and we do not need to search our hearts every time we go to the shops for food. But the unusual, the large purchases need to be examined carefully to make sure that we are spending 'for the love of God'. This is the Bahá'í standard.

Economy

Content thyself with but little of this world's goods! Verily, economy is a great treasure.[5]

Be not grieved if the trash of the world is decreased in thy hands . . .[6]

Economy implies using money, materials, etc., to the best advantage. There are at least three important reasons for being economical: (1) low income; (2) the foolishness of wasting the natural resources of the earth, as well as things that human time and energy have made; (3) the desire to share with others.

I have occasionally heard Bahá'ís speak as though they looked down on small savings. But these in time add up to a considerable amount; and they also show that the individual does not have a wasteful attitude. One should ask oneself questions such as these: Do I waste food by unwise buying, or by permitting it to spoil? Do I waste electricity by leaving lights on in rooms that are not in use, or by letting radio or television programmes continue in empty rooms? As a family do we carelessly leave toys, bicycles, tools, etc. out of doors, where the rain may ruin them? Do I frequently wear clothing which is not suitable for the work I am doing; for instance, my best suede shoes when I set out bulbs in a wet garden?

True economy requires knowledge, the use of good judgement, and the balancing of values. If I am buying a winter coat I need to know the comparative warmth and strength of different woollen materials and coat linings. I should judge whether a coat that looks well on me will be suitable for the varied occasions on which I need to wear it. Is the colour so light that I will have to spend an unreasonable amount on cleaning bills? Let us suppose that I find a coat that I judge to be warm, lasting, good-looking, and suitable, but it costs thirty dollars more than I had planned to spend. By cutting down my contributions to the Bahá'í Fund by five dollars a month for six months I can make up the extra sum. It is my scale of values, material and spiritual, which will determine whether or not I buy the coat.

Sometimes it is more economical to spend money than to keep it. Here one has to make a judgement as to whether saving or spending is more useful, being careful to guard against decisions influenced by immediate personal liking and comfort. Illustrations from everyday life include questions such as: Shall I save time and strength by taking a bus instead of walking? Will the time spent in mending this worn garment be so great that it is wiser to buy a new one? Will the large repairs needed on my old car cost so much that it is more economical to buy another?

Women, perhaps more than men, often have to decide whether a garment is too 'out of style' to be worn in public. Bahá'ís have this interesting statement by Bahá'u'lláh to help them in their decisions:

> The choice of clothing. . . [is] left to the discretion of men. But beware, O people, lest ye make

yourselves the playthings of the ignorant.
[That is, do not make yourselves objects of ridicule.] [7]

Extravagance

The dictionary defines extravagance as 'exceeding prudence or necessity in expenditure; wasteful.' It implies going to extremes in the use of money and materials. Some people are extravagant because of poor judgement. For others, spending large sums of money seems to build up their feeling of status, their sense of being valuable human beings. For a third group the possession of many unnecessary things makes them feel superior; they like to impress others with these evidences of greater wealth, and so 'exalt themselves'.

The Bahá'í teachings concerning extravagance are indicated in the following quotations.

> . . . take heed not to outstrip the bounds of moderation, and be numbered among the extravagant. [8]

> Deal with them with undeviating justice, so that none among them may either suffer want, or be pampered with luxuries. [9]

> [To the Pope Bahá'u'lláh wrote,] Sell all the embellished ornaments thou dost possess, and expend them in the path of God . . . [10]

From the material side, the evil in extravagance is that it keeps out of circulation money and materials which could be better used elsewhere. From the spiritual viewpoint, it indicates careless thinking, or even self-love.

We should remind ourselves that a purchase which is an extravagance for Jane may be a necessity for Mary, and therefore be very slow to label another as 'terribly extravagant'. Moreover, each individual should have the freedom to budget his own money as he sees fit. If I choose to do my own laundry in order to have money for buying books I should not be criticized.

Hoarding

The person who hoards may also be extravagant, but this is not always true. The hoarder is distrustful of the future; he thinks, 'I don't need these things now, but the future is so uncertain, and I may need them sometime.' Hoarding is often the result of living in great poverty as a child, and one should feel sympathy with those who have been so deprived. But we should try to help this type of hoarder realize that he does not have to be in bondage to his past.

Some who remember the hoarding of food during the Second World War may say, 'But I never hoarded! It just was not right to do so.' Are you sure you do not hoard now? How much clothing that you very seldom wear is stored in your wardrobes? Do you know anyone who *needs* it?

Mary Hanford Ford, in *The Oriental Rose,* told a story about 'Abdu'l-Bahá which illustrates His ideas about economy and hoarding. His wife thought that when He entertained the Governor of 'Akká He should wear a more handsome coat than He usually wore. So she ordered a better coat made by the tailor, and substituted it for the one 'Abdu'l-Bahá had been wearing. He noticed the difference in the coat at once, and exclaimed, 'Where is my coat? Some one has left me a coat that is not mine!' His wife tried to explain why he should have the more expensive coat, but He was not convinced.

'For the price of this coat you can buy five such as I ordinarily use, and do you think I would spend so much money upon a coat which only I shall wear? If you think I need a new one, very well, but send this back and have the tailor make me for this price five such as I usually have. Then you see, I shall not only have a new one, but I shall also have four to give to others!'[11]

Stinginess

The stingy person objects to a fair sharing; he is meanly unjust. Do you know a family where the father decides how the income is to be spent, and doles it out bit by bit, except when he wants something for his own pleasure? Do you know a man who consistently tries to underpay and overwork his employees? Or a person who 'forgets' to pay the pledge he has made to a charitable organization?

Overstep not the bounds of moderation, and deal justly with them that serve thee.[12]

The people of Bahá [Bahá'ís] should not deny any soul the reward due to him. . .[13]

Another expression of stinginess is the giving of a gift with the clear implication that services are expected in return: services which require the expenditure of time and energy worth four or five times the cost of the gift.

Sharing Expenses

If four friends are going to a restaurant for dinner, it seems obvious that each should know before they start whether one is inviting the others to dinner, or whether each is to pay for his own meal. Yet often this is not clear, and one or more are embarrassed when the bill appears.

Bahá'ís often do things together which involve the spending of money, and there should be definite agreement on the sharing of the expenses. If there is one member of a group who has more money than the others, should he offer to pay more than his share? Probably not, except in a case of immediate need. Certainly he should do nothing which will make his friends feel poverty-stricken. Regardless of how much money a person has, he should not embarrass others by always insisting that he pay the taxi fare, the bill for coffee, or the expenses of the committee luncheon.

Accuracy in money-matters helps to prevent misunderstanding. If one person collects the money for the luncheon bill, make sure that he is not left to pay the tips for everyone. If a group of four go to a restaurant for refreshments after a meeting, the person who has only a cup of coffee should not be expected to pay one-fourth of the total bill, when each of the others has had coffee, a sandwich, and ice cream!

If you feel that most of these comments on sharing expenses are hardly worth making, remember that many small injustices may be more distressing than a single large one. Ten mosquito bites may be more painful than a quick, sharp bite from your neighbour's dog!

Within a group of friends it should be possible for one to say, without a feeling of humiliation, 'I am sorry but I cannot afford to do what you are suggesting.' It need not be said with the kind of aggressiveness which makes the others feel it is their fault that you do not have the money, and your friends will probably respect you more than if you make up several reasons to avoid the truth.

Contributions

Bahá'ís look forward to a future in which there will be very few people in serious financial need. Until that time they are urged to contribute as generously as possible to needy individuals, not directly to those who beg on the street, but those whom one *knows* to be in real need.

> If ye encounter one who is poor, treat him not disdainfully.[14]

Be generous in prosperity, and thankful in adversity.[15]

Be ye a rich treasure to every indigent one . . .[16]

No deed of man is greater before God than helping the poor.[17]

In addition to gifts to needy individuals, many people contribute to one or more worthy causes, such as the Red Cross, hospitals, the SPCA, Boy Scouts, etc. Bahá'ís may contribute to such needs. but feel that their first responsibility is to the Bahá'í Fund, which supports the varied and far-flung activities of the Faith.

Wealth is praiseworthy in the highest degree, if it is acquired by an individual's own efforts and the grace of God, in commerce, agriculture, art and industry, and if it be expended for philanthropic purposes.[18]

The problem of how much one should give to individuals and organizations is difficult, and each person should make this decision for himself. It seems evident that one should not neglect needed visits to doctor and dentist in order to contribute to the Bahá'í Fund. Should I give so generously that I am likely to become a financial burden on others? This seems to imply some injustice to those who will have to provide my support. But the following statements by Shoghi Effendi, Guardian of the Bahá'í Faith, should cause Bahá'ís to question whether they are giving too much attention to future financial security.

We must be like the fountain or spring that is continually emptying itself of all that it has and is continually being refilled from an invisible source. To be continually giving out for the good of our fellows undeterred by the fear of poverty and reliant on the unfailing bounty of the Source of all wealth and all good — this is the secret of right living.[19]

Contributions to this fund constitute, in addition, a practical and effective way whereby every believer can test the measure and character of his faith, and to prove in deeds the intensity of his devotion and attachment to the Cause. . . .[20]

Shoghi Effendi also gives a clear statement of one obligation which comes before giving to the Bahá'í Fund.

Our debts, however, should be considered as sacred and take precedence over any other thing (i.e. payment of debts comes before contributions to the Cause) for upon this principle does the foundation of our economic life rest.[21]

It seems probable that this statement about the payment of debts was not intended to apply to regular loans from banks and similar organizations, which are a recognized part of our economic life and are to be repaid over a period of time, or by instalments.

My own experience and observation lead me to think that a loan to an individual Bahá'í should be made through the Local Spiritual Assembly. Another Bahá'í may provide the money for the loan, but if it is made through the Assembly the transaction is recorded in the minutes, and some borrowers will feel greater responsibility for prompt repayment. Moreover, it might save both lender and borrower considerable embarrassment.

The spirit in which one makes a contribution is of the utmost importance. If one gives grudgingly, and afterwards resents having given, it would have been better to leave the money in one's own pocket! Give joyfully, out of devotion to a great purpose.

Collections of Books, Records, Art Objects, etc.

A person's profession often makes it necessary for him to buy many books, or records, or photographs, or a variety of art objects. In addition, many people who have enough money to do so make collections for other reasons; for example − (1) to add to their own knowledge, enjoyment, and inspiration; (2) to share them with others; or (3) to make themselves feel 'superior', or 'cultured'.

No true Bahá'í will make expensive collections in order to increase his feeling of superiority over others.

Bahá'u'lláh's 'prescription for living' gives an important place to the arts and sciences, and therefore Bahá'ís with a considerable income may feel justified in spending money on collections of books, paintings, etc., provided they have met their responsibilities to the Bahá'í Fund, and only to the extent that they share their treasures with others.

*　　*　　*

'Lord! Pitiful are we, grant us Thy Favour; poor, bestow upon us a share from the Ocean of Thy Wealth; needy, do Thou satisfy us; abased, give us Thy Glory. The fowls of the air and the beasts of the field receive their meat each day from Thee and all beings partake of Thy care and loving-kindness.

'Deprive not this feeble one from Thy wondrous Grace and vouchsafe by Thy Might unto this helpless soul Thy Bounty.

'Give us our daily bread and grant Thy increase in the necessities of life, that we may be dependent on none other but Thee, may commune wholly with Thee, may walk in Thy ways and declare Thy mysteries. Thou art the Almighty and the Loving and the Provider of all mankind.'

'Abdu'l-Bahá

7

THE DEVELOPMENT OF ARTS AND SCIENCES

IN THE BAHÁ'Í teachings art and science are given great importance; they are reflections of the Sun of Truth, of the Word of God. Each individual must make an effort to become a creative contributor in some art or science; or, if he is unable to produce something 'new' in art or science, he must use creatively the work of others. The person whose whole life is based on imitation is half dead; he is not 'alive' mentally or spiritually. We have already quoted 'Abdu'l-Bahá's statement that 'The investigating mind is attentive, alive; the mind callous and indifferent is deaf and dead' (See chapter 5).

The sun of Truth is the Word of God upon which dependeth the education of those who are endowed with the power of understanding and of utterance. It is the true spirit and the heavenly water, through whose aid and gracious providence all things have been and will be quickened. Its appearance in every mirror is conditioned by the colour of that mirror. For instance, when its light is cast upon the mirrors of the hearts of the wise, it bringeth forth wisdom. In like manner when it manifesteth itself in the mirrors of the hearts of craftsmen, it unfoldeth new and unique arts, and when reflected in the hearts of those that apprehend the truth it revealeth wondrous tokens of true knowledge and discloseth the verities of God's utterance.[1]

Great indeed is the claim of scientists and craftsmen on the peoples of the world.[2]

Woe to those who are contented with ignorance, whose hearts are gladdened by thoughtless imitation, . . . who have wasted their lives![3]

. . . in this new century the attainment of science, arts and *belles lettres,* whether divine or worldly, material or spiritual, is a matter which is acceptable before God and a duty which is incumbent upon us to accomplish. Therefore, never deny the spiritual things to the material, rather both are incumbent upon thee. Nevertheless, at the time when thou art working for such a scientific attainment, thou must be controlled by the attraction of the love of thy Glorious Lord and mindful of mentioning His splendid Name. This being the case, thou must attain the art thou art studying to its perfection.[4]

The Creative Individual

Many readers of the above may say, 'But I am not a creative person! I am not a genius; I am just an average human being.' The Bahá'í who has meditated on the first quotation above should ask himself, 'Am I willing to forgo making full use of this 'heavenly water'? If not, how can I learn to use it creatively?'

A. The development of creativity

The person who wishes to become more creative will

be helped if he first gains some understanding of the genesis of the creative process. As early as the age of two years some children give evidence of real creative power, while others show the characteristics of the conformist, the imitator. What is the cause of this difference?

Each individual, except the most feeble-minded, is endowed at birth with a certain amount of creative energy, an ability to make something *new* out of the elements of the environment in which he finds himself. How much the amount varies from individual to individual we do not know, for so many of us actually use so little of this ability to change the world. Our failure to do so is not due to the fact that 'man is naturally lazy'; it has its roots in our mistaken ideas of how to train and educate young children.

The baby, except when ill, is never inert! Each waking hour is filled with activity: he kicks and squeals, he cries or smiles, he pushes against the side of his crib, he shakes the rattle or throws it on the floor. He listens to the voices about him, and begins to know the difference between the tone which says, 'Food is coming', and the one which says, 'Now go to sleep.' At the same time he is increasing his skill in focusing his eyes on objects, and in selecting details which differentiate his mother from other human beings. Similarly, other sensations which come to him from the outside world are gradually perceived as different from one another, and out of the 'blooming, buzzing confusion' of early babyhood he begins to create his own 'meanings', his own ideas of what objects and people are like. As his ability to move about increases, he acquires other sensations which he incorporates into the earlier meanings, and thus gradually changes them. He begins to do things with the objects around him; he rolls the ball, he pushes the small box, he tips the cup and watches the milk run along the table. Each of these experiences adds to the meanings which he is creating for himself.

The baby also discovers very early in life that what he does makes a difference to the way people treat him. He learns whether crying after he has been put to bed will bring someone rushing to his side, or whether his tears will be ignored. He discovers the use of smiles and laughter in compelling the pleased attention of his family. From these and many other experiences, he adds to his understanding of human beings.

But the young child discovers very early in his life that there are limits to the experiments that he can make on his own body, and on the objects and people around him. These limits are sometimes imposed by the nature of the inanimate things in his environment; but the ones which have the greatest influence on him are due to the behaviour of adults. He learns that some of his explorations are received by an emphatic 'No!' This no is often accompanied by angry tones, frowns, a slap on the hand, or a spank. To other explorations his parents say 'Yes!' and this yes may be emphasized by smiles, pleased comments, kisses, and other evidence of satisfaction.

If the child is sufficiently active, he tends to disregard many of the noes which people and things say to him, or he learns to experiment in ways which do not get him into trouble. If he is less active, his experimentation decreases, and he tends to repeat the behaviour to which adults say yes. Occasionally we find a child who has been so frustrated by the preponderance of noes in his environment that he appears to be feeble-minded. Such a child can be re-trained to greater activity only by a change in the behaviour of adults; his smallest achievement must, for a time, be received with great praise, and use of the frustrating no must be avoided as much as possible.

All children create for themselves many incomplete and mistaken meanings. The child who is allowed to experiment rather freely corrects many of these meanings almost automatically, as he explores more aspects of his world. Other mistakes are corrected by the noes of objects and people, provided that these come in a way that does not seriously decrease his courage. Indeed, the discovery of what behaviour produces the yes or the no is one goal of his experimentation. But the child who is continually frustrated by a high percentage of noes has less opportunity to correct his mistaken meanings; he becomes not only less creative, but also more confused and distorted in the little he does create.

No child can grow up to be a useful member of an organized community without occasionally experiencing the frustrating 'No!' But most parents use this word or its equivalents much more frequently than is necessary or desirable. A considerable part of successful parenthood lies in the provision of an environment in which it is less often necessary to say no. This means, first, the elimination of objects which he must not touch. Second, it means the provision of simple materials which he can use for creative activity. Large blocks or a set of small blocks which he can build into a 'house', coloured crayons and large sheets of cheap paper, a lump of clay, hammer and nails and boards, blunt scissors and paste: all of these are much better gifts for a child of five or six than 'toys' which can be used in only one or two ways.

The child in his early years should be encouraged to combine these raw materials in any way he chooses. Occasionally an adult may work beside the child, building or making some object with the same material the child is using. But if the child shows any tendency to copy slavishly the adult's work, this working together should be discontinued until the child acquires more faith in his own ability to create.

Experimentation with words, sounds, tones, and with movements of his own body, should also be encouraged. As the child grows older, he may need some more direct instruction in the techniques of using saw or plane, paintbrush or drumstick. The danger here is that one might make the child feel that the product of his work must be like that of other children or adults. The child who combines words, colours, or sounds — and bits of wood, metal, or cloth — in *new* ways is likely to become the creative adult of the future.

The creative process, then, begins in the sensing and perceiving of the physical world and of human beings, and in the building of meanings with regard to their many aspects. The creative individual has the desire and the courage to experiment, to try new combinations of the perceptions and images and emotions which arise from his direct contact with the world around him. He has many curiosities, he delights in the new and the untried. He is not held back by fear of his own emotions, of what others will say or do in criticism of his work. Such courage is related to the whole structure of the personality, and we have indicated ways in which it is dependent on the experiences of early childhood.

Many adults have not had the kind of education described above. They have to re-educate themselves, if they would become more creative.

B. *Different kinds of creativity*

The creator in any field of art begins with the purpose of stating something which is to him vital and striking. This purpose may at first be rather vague, but as he plays with it, it begins to take on more exact definition. He starts his search for the symbols — combinations of words, colours, or sounds — which will make his feeling, his idea, a living thing, able to stir in others a keen awareness of some aspect of the world.

Out of his past experience — the odour and colour of a flower, the sound of water in a mountain brook, the swaying of birch trees in the wind; memories of his first day at school, his first adolescent love, or last year's struggle to earn money for food and rent — from all of his experience comes drifting or surging in a wealth of symbols. He cannot compel the right one to come, but he can pursue trains of association, hoping to find the one he needs, perhaps having to wait patiently while a whole series of unwanted images flow through him. The touchstone by which he accepts or rejects each symbol is its ability to convey his particular meaning. And this meaning, this purpose, possesses him more and more completely as he strives to embody it. Hours may pass, but to him there is only the present creative moment.

When the creative work is moving swiftly and surely, the goal seems to act as a magnet which pulls to itself the appropriate symbol, and the creator may be only half-conscious of the ones which the 'magnet' rejects.

In the field of *invention* the goal is conceived in terms of practical use. The elements which will compose the new machine or appliance are selected in terms of this goal, as in the case of artistic creation, but the symbol plays a less important part in the process, and the elements combined are wheels and cogs, cylinders and wires. The final test of the creative process is whether the machine works in actual use, while in the arts the test of success is found in the joy and the enhancement of life which the artist's creation gives to himself and others.

Creativity in human relationships is dependent on the ability to perceive the real needs and desires of others, and this is impossible for the person who is wholly concerned with his own likes and dislikes, or with his will to exert power over others. Convention, tradition, and allegiance to outworn social institutions hamper man in finding new solutions to the problems of human communities. Here, as in all other fields, courage to try the untried is an essential element in creative behaviour.

C. How to become more creative

From this brief summary, we may come to some conclusions about what an individual needs to do in order to become more creative, and to contribute more to the problems and needs of today. He should first ask himself whether he is vividly aware of all the material world about him: sights, sounds, tastes, odours, and the feeling of the movement of his own body. If not, he can train himself to be more perceptive, realizing how important this is to art, science, and industry. He can also train himself to see more clearly the behaviour and aims of other human beings, even though this means that he must learn to be less self-centred.

Secondly, he must train himself to be aware of the occasions when fear of disapproval, or of the forces of tradition, causes him to discard new and better ways of working, or of dealing with men and women. As he becomes more conscious of the many times that lack of courage inhibits creative behaviour, he may gradually become dissatisfied with a life so filled with fear, and begin to make an effort to put some of his good ideas into practice.

Thirdly, the person who is striving to become more creative can seriously study his own desires and aims, in order to decide which ones are really worth creative endeavour. He may select one such aim, and try to clarify it, so that he becomes more keenly aware of just what is needed to bring about the results he desires. The more vividly he can imagine the desired result, the greater the probability that he will be able to select the elements which will create the solution or the product.

Fourthly, he can form the habit of experimentation, whether in science or art or human relationships. He can learn to use his goal as a magnet to select elements that are in accord with his purpose, and to reject patiently elements which are irrelevant or inadequate.

He can try out tentative solutions in various ways. Does the machine do the job as well as he hoped it would? Does the painting, or essay, or dance give him a deep satisfaction and sense of well-being? Does it give evidence of conveying his feeling and thought to others? Does his experiment in human relations increase co-operation and happiness among his family, friends, or acquaintances?

If his solution proves unsatisfactory, he can learn

to try again; he can realize that attitudes of discouragement and defeat destroy energy, and have no place in the life of the creative individual.

Every Bahá'í feels the obligation to contribute to the life of the community in which he lives, and he conceives of the community as gradually widening to include all human life on this earth. Even though the work by which he earns his livelihood may be largely repetitive, as in a factory for example, he realizes that in human relationships and in activities outside working hours he has wide scope for the creation of new skills, new forms of art or craft, more satisfying methods of association. He is therefore eager to become more creative in the use of his energy and he welcomes all the creative efforts of others which are conducive to fellowship, unity, and happiness among men.

The Source of Inspiration

This discussion of the creative process has not sufficiently taken into account the *source* of power, of inspiration, which, as we read in the first quotation in this chapter, is the Sun of Truth, the Word of God.

> Through the mere revelation of the word 'Fashioner', issuing forth from His lips and proclaiming His attribute to mankind, such power is released as can generate, through successive ages, all the manifold arts which the hands of man can produce.[5]

Through prayer and meditation the Bahá'í prepares

himself so that this great Power may flow through him. It permeates his purposes, it frees him from tradition and repetition, it fires him with the will to become creative.

We know that the creative Word of God comes to us through the great Divine Educators: in this age through the Báb and Bahá'u'lláh. We are also told that this Power is directed towards us by spiritually developed souls who have left this earth-life. How this is accomplished we do not know, but it is certainly not through the 'voices' of the spiritualist's seance, or similar phenomena. Bahá'u'lláh Himself assures us that part of the work of those who have 'remained faithful to the Cause of God' is to mediate inspiration to those who are working creatively on this planet.

> The soul that hath remained faithful to the Cause of God, and stood unwaveringly firm in His Path shall, after his ascension, be possessed of such power that all the worlds which the Almighty hath created can benefit through him. Such a soul provideth, at the bidding of the Ideal King and Divine Educator, the pure leaven that leaveneth the world of being, and furnisheth the power through which the arts and wonders of the world are made manifest.[6]

The Purposes Served by the Arts and Sciences

Attainment of the arts and sciences is described by 'Abdu'l-Bahá as a duty which Bahá'ís must accomplish. Why do these fields of endeavour have such importance? What purposes do they serve?

Art and science, each in its own way, add to the beauty of our lives, and beauty is a divine characteristic. One of the frequently used titles of Bahá'u'lláh is the Blessed Beauty. The Writings of both Bahá'u'lláh and 'Abdu'l-Bahá are filled with symbols based on the beauties of the natural world. In *The Hidden Words,* Arabic, no. 36, Bahá'u'lláh directs man to 'mirror forth' His Beauty. Through the arts and sciences, through 'patient lives of active service', through prayer, man strives to express this beauty.

A student once asked 'Abdu'l-Bahá whether he should give up his studies in Paris in order to devote all his time to teaching the Bahá'í Faith. 'Abdu'l-Bahá replied that it would be better to do both, and added that the practice of an art leads to sociability, that is, to fellowship and unity. Friendliness among individuals is a prerequisite for the unity of mankind. Art and science can transcend national boundaries; they have an international language of their own.

> The source of crafts, sciences and arts is the power of reflection. Make ye every effort that out of this ideal mine there may gleam forth such pearls of wisdom and utterance as will promote the well-being and harmony of all the kindreds of the earth.[7]

> How shall we utilize these gifts and expend these bounties? By directing our efforts toward the unification of the human race.[8]

> The results of scientific investigation, if rightly used, safeguard and protect man; they enable him to

predict many aspects of the future. The Bahá'í Writings emphasize the importance of careful scientific research.

> God has endowed man with intelligence so that he may safeguard and protect himself. Therefore he must provide and surround himself with all that scientific skill can produce. He must be deliberate, thoughtful and thorough in his purposes . . .[9]

In 1912 in Washington, D.C., 'Abdu'l-Bahá gave a remarkable talk on the importance of science, from which we quote at some length.

> The virtues of humanity are many but science is the most noble of them all. . . . It is a bestowal of God; it is not material, it is divine. . . . All the powers and attributes of man are human and hereditary in origin, outcomes of nature's processes, except the intellect, which is super-natural. . . .
> Science is the first emanation from God toward man. All created beings embody the potentiality of material perfection, but the power of intellectual investigation and scientific acquisition is a higher virtue specialized to man alone. . . .
> All blessings are divine in origin but none can be compared with this power of intellectual investigation and research which is an eternal gift producing fruits of unending delight. . . . Therefore you should put forward your most earnest efforts toward the acquisition of science and arts. . . . A scientific man is a true index and representative of humanity, for through processes of inductive reasoning and research he is informed of all that appertains to humanity, its status, conditions and happenings.[10]

Teaching is Both an Art and a Science

Good teaching of any subject-matter is both an art and a science. In the case of teaching the Bahá'í Faith to an enquirer, we find, first, that there are scientific principles of learning and teaching which will make our work more effective. Among them are the following:

1. Respect the learner. Respect implies courtesy. Never bully, even in polite ways. Never try to compel acceptance of your ideas.

2. A Bahá'í teacher must really value the learner as a human being; as a friend, not just a potential convert.

3. Make a serious, imaginative effort to understand the desires of the learner. Let him empty himself of his problems and express his interests, before you try to give him your ideas.

4. Adjust the material presented to the learner's capacity. Teach first what he can accept easily. Proceed as slowly — or as rapidly — as necessary.

5. When repetition is necessary, approach facts or ideas from many angles; use varied illustrations of a single principle. Make abstract ideas concrete, through illustration, analogy, etc.

6. When presenting factual material, be accurate. Avoid pseudo-science.

7. When you present material concerned with habits and attitudes, strive to exemplify these in your own life.

8. Avoid being too 'helpful', in ways the learner does not wish to be helped.

9. Beware of enjoying the feeling of power over others. The teacher should not teach in order to gain emotional satisfaction, though such satisfaction may be a by-product.

The *art* of teaching the Faith includes the development of sensitivity to the interests and needs of the enquirer. We must strive to see his world through his eyes, to enter into his feelings and thoughts with understanding. We must develop insight to help us choose the words which will appeal to him, which will not antagonize him. With one person we may use symbols from the world of nature to convey spiritual meanings; with another, comparisons from chemistry or physics will be more effective. Through analysis of our teaching experiences we should develop a 'sixth sense' as to what to say to each learner. This does not mean that we neglect the inspiration we receive through prayer; we unite that with use of the abilities to feel and understand, which God has given us.

In conclusion, let us remember that the builders of the new World Order are those who have the courage to experiment. Bahá'u'lláh has given us basic principles; it is our responsibility to *apply them creatively*.

8

EDUCATION IN THE HOME

THE PURPOSE OF this and the following chapter is to present the basic Bahá'í teachings with regard to the importance of education, and also some specific statements about curricula and methods of teaching which were made by 'Abdu'l-Bahá in letters and lectures. All of this material should be considered in the light of the earlier chapters, each of which has been concerned with some aspect of the educative process.

In passages such as the following, Bahá'u'lláh stresses the necessity for education, and the importance of knowledge.

> Knowledge is as wings to man's life, and a ladder for his ascent. Its acquisition is incumbent upon everyone. . . .
> In truth, knowledge is a veritable treasure for man, and a source of glory, of bounty, of joy, of exaltation, of cheer and gladness unto him.[1]

> Everyone, whether man or woman, should hand over to a trusted person a portion of what he or she earneth through trade, agriculture or other occupation, for the training and education of children . . .[2]

> Schools must first train the children in the prin-

ciples of religion. . . . But this in such a measure that it may not injure the children by resulting in ignorant fanaticism and bigotry.[3]

'Abdu'l-Bahá presents the need for education and knowledge in greater detail.

> . . . knowledge is the most glorious gift of man, and the most noble of human perfections. To oppose knowledge is ignorant, and he who detests knowledge and science is not a man, but rather an animal without intelligence. For knowledge is light, life, felicity, perfection, beauty, and the means of approaching the Threshold of Unity. It is the honour and glory of the world of humanity, and the greatest bounty of God. . . .
>
> Happy are those who spend their days in gaining knowledge, in discovering the secrets of nature, and in penetrating the subtleties of pure truth! Woe to those who are contented with ignorance, whose hearts are gladdened by thoughtless imitation, who have fallen into the lowest depths of ignorance and foolishness, and who have wasted their lives![4]

> But education is of three kinds: material, human, and spiritual. Material education is concerned with the progress and development of the body, through gaining its sustenance, its material comfort and ease. . . .
>
> Human education signifies civilization and progress: that is to say, government, administration, charitable works, trades, arts and handicrafts, sciences, great inventions and discoveries of physical laws, which are the activities essential to man. . . .

Divine education is that of the Kingdom of God: it consists in acquiring divine perfections, and this is true education. . . This is the supreme goal of the world of humanity.[5]

Mother and father are the first educators of a child, and in the early months of babyhood the role of the mother is the more important. She gives the baby his first experience of a loving human being. If her voice is soft and pleasant, if she handles the baby gently, if she meets his need for food without much delay, he will begin to learn that people are loving, friendly, and trustworthy. In the Bahá'í Faith much stress is put on the education of girls, in order that they may be prepared to be loving, understanding, and intelligent mothers.

As the baby grows a little older the father should enter more and more into the child's experience, so that the child realizes that there are others, in addition to his mother, who are kind and helpful. Gradually the number of people who have intimate contact with him increases, and if all of them are friendly he begins to move towards them with assurance and interest. This training in outgoing friendliness begins much earlier than many people think. Obviously the baby could not put into words what he is learning, but his feelings and awakening mind are given a direction which will later become an attitude of love and co-operation.

. . . in this New Cycle, education and training are recorded in the Book of God as obligatory and not voluntary. That is, it is enjoined upon the father and mother, as a duty, to strive with all effort to train the daughter and the son, to nurse them from the breast of knowledge and to rear them in the bosom of sciences and arts. . . .

. . . If it be considered through the eye of reality, the training and culture of daughters is more necessary than that of sons, for these girls will come to the station of motherhood and will mould the lives of the children. The first trainer of the child is the mother. . . .

. . . Endeavour with heart, with life, to train your children, especially the daughters. No excuse is acceptable in this matter.[6]

Love and understanding between the parents is essential to the education of children in the home. If there is conflict between mother and father, the child, even before he can talk, will sense this and will react with feelings of distress and insecurity. The most important gift which parents can give a child is their deep and understanding love for one another, for from it he begins to learn the meaning of unselfish and happy devotion.

If love and agreement are manifest in a single family, that family will advance, become illumined and spiritual; but if enmity and hatred exist within it destruction and dispersion are inevitable.[7]

Young children learn with great speed from the example of the behaviour of others: witness the ease with which they take on the local habits of intonation of voice, pronunciation of words, and rhythms of speech. The three-year-old girl talks to her doll as her mother has spoken to her. The four-year-old boy may already have copied his father's mannerisms and posture.

> Education must be considered as most important; for as diseases in the world of bodies are extremely contagious, so, in the same way, qualities of spirit and heart are extremely contagious.[8]

The forms of courtesy which are approved in a neighbourhood are best learned through imitating the example of older children and adults. If a child loves and admires his mother and father he will *want* to imitate their speech and manners. Occasionally he may be reminded to say 'Please' and 'Thank you', but it probably does not help the learning process to constantly 'nag' him in such matters. Of course parents must show real courtesy to the child as well as to one another. An older boy or girl may be helped by learning one of Bahá'u'lláh's statements about courtesy.

> I admonish you to observe courtesy. For above all else it is the prince of virtues.... Whoso is endued with courtesy hath indeed attained a sublime station.[9]

> Courtesy, is, in truth, a raiment which fitteth all men, whether young or old. Well is it with him that adorneth his temple therewith...[10]

Each member of a family has both rights and responsibilities. Children have the right to loving care and training in the home; they have the right to be respected as human beings, and to have freedom to develop their own special abilities.

It is evident that in a true Bahá'í family no member can be a dictator, for the use of any kind of compulsion destroys the unity of the family. In some cultures we find that it is still expected that the father shall be the source of final authority, the 'boss'. If a man with this tradition becomes a Bahá'í he must change his behaviour to meet the standard of co-operation between all family members. This is not an easy change to make, but the father (or mother) who continues to be a dictator should not be surprised if the children later reject the Bahá'í teachings, for they have not found the Bahá'í principles of consultation and fellowship in their own home.

Many families find it useful to have a weekly meeting of parents and older children, in which they consult on any problems that have arisen and make plans for the coming week. Other families have such a conference only when an important decision is to be made. Frequent consultation in the family is a great help in building a useful, happy life for parents and children.

> All the virtues must be taught the family. The integrity of the family bond must be constantly considered and the rights of the individual members must not be transgressed. The rights of the son, the father, the mother, none of them must be transgressed, none of them must be arbitrary. Just

as the son has certain obligations to his father, the father likewise has certain obligations to his son. The mother, the sister and other members of the household have their certain prerogatives. All these rights and prerogatives must be conserved, yet the unity of the family must be sustained.[11]

In cases where other members of the household include a maid or a cleaning-woman, children should be taught to be courteous to this helper, and not to waste her time by making unnecessary work for her. Teenagers in a Bahá'í home should realize that they have a responsibility to show, by their considerate and helpful behaviour, the ideals of Bahá'í character.

As soon as he is physically capable, the young child should be given small responsibilities in the maintenance of the life of the home. These should be presented to him as a privilege: 'All of us do things to help, and now you are old enough to join in.' As the boy or girl grows older these responsibilities should be increased, but care should be taken that these jobs are not always the most tedious and unpleasant ones. Both pleasant and unpleasant tasks should be rotated among the members of the family.

Parents who truly love a child will not pamper him by permitting him to be always the 'centre of the stage', or to be a nuisance or a hindrance to others. The pampered child's area of activity is too limited, because he is not allowed to solve the simple problems which are appropriate for his age. Later, especially when he first goes to school, he finds that others of his age are more capable than he is, and he frequently retreats from the social and intellectual problems he meets, or he may become a trouble-maker in an effort to draw attention away from his incompetence.

Harshness, strictness, or neglect are as much out of place in the life of a child as is pampering. The harsh parent is teaching his children that the world is an unkind and unfriendly place, and that adults should be distrusted. These attitudes are obviously not those of human beings who are eager to build a world of peace and co-operation.

> The child must not be oppressed or censured because it is undeveloped; it must be patiently trained.[12]

Bahá'í parents understand that one of their first responsibilities is to teach their children the love of God and of the great Messengers He has sent to the world. Mother and father speak naturally and simply of spiritual matters, such as prayer; their daily lives are characterized by trust in God and by joy in all He has given them. In such an atmosphere the child's understanding gradually increases, and he shares more and more in the family's spiritual purposes and activity. The example of the lives of their parents should show children that true faith is evidenced more by deeds than by words, and that any real religion must result in kind and friendly behaviour.

> I give you my advice and it is this: Train these children with divine exhortations. From their

childhood instil in their hearts the love of God so they may manifest in their lives the fear of God and have confidence in the bestowals of God. Teach them to free themselves from human imperfections and to acquire the divine perfections latent in the heart of man. The life of man is useful if he attains the perfections of man. If he becomes the centre of the imperfections of the world of humanity, death is better than life, and non-existence better than existence. Therefore make ye an effort in order that these children may be rightly trained and educated and that each one of them may attain perfection in the world of humanity.[13]

Children need times to be alone. This will help them to avoid excessive dependence on others. It gives them time to think their own thoughts, free from the presence and pressures of older people. It is an essential preparation for adult prayer and meditation. It provides opportunity for the types of creative project which require concentration of attention: drawing, painting, woodworking, etc. Many children and young people think that co-operation requires that one be in the physical presence of other people. They should be helped to understand that any activity which contributes to the welfare and happiness of others is co-operative behaviour. For example, the child of eight who stays alone in his own room for an hour to write a poem for his mother's birthday is engaged in a co-operative project.

Whoso reciteth, in the privacy of his chamber, the verses revealed by God, the scattering angels of the Almighty shall scatter abroad the fragrance of the words uttered by his mouth, and shall cause the heart of every righteous man to throb. Though he may, at first, remain unaware of its effect, yet the virtue of the grace vouchsafed unto him must needs sooner or later exercise its influence upon his soul.[14]

Gentleness and patience are essential in the training and education of children. 'Abdu'l-Bahá emphasized this in the following charming comparison, reported by a pilgrim: 'If a wise father plays with his children, who has a right to say that it is not good for them? He calls them to come to him as the hen calls her chicks; he knows that they are little and must be coaxed along – coaxed along, because they are young and tiny.'

Reward and punishment constitute another important factor. Bahá'u'lláh has called them the 'twin pillars' which uphold the social order of the world. And psychologists come to a similar conclusion: their experiments show that the individual learns when he feels satisfaction accompanying the desirable response, and dissatisfaction accompanying the undesirable response. In applying these principles to the teaching of children in the home, it is important that the child who is rewarded knows *specifically* what he has done that is 'right' or 'good'. It is even more important that he understands exactly what behaviour has brought a punishment. (Punishment should be understood to mean any words or actions which cause the child to be dissatisfied, which he feels as unpleasant. This may range from his father's statement, 'I am disappointed that you were so unkind to your brother', to deprivation of a trip to the country which the child very much wished to take. Children differ greatly in what they find satisfying or dissatisfying, and therefore rewards and punishments must be selected in terms of each individual's preferences.)

Experimental studies have shown that a child learns most rapidly of all when the 'right' response brings a reward and a 'wrong' response some form of dissatisfaction. The second most effective condition in producing learning is reward with no punishment. The third is no reward for the right response, but punishment for the wrong. When the child is neither rewarded nor punished, very little if any learning occurs. Parents should be sure that they reward the right response whenever it is made, and do not fall into the habit of ignoring the right, but always punishing the wrong.

When a child has done his best, he should be encouraged, even if the result has been inadequate. With help, he will probably do better next time. Both children and parents should understand that 'a mistake is a friendly invitation to try again' (Alfred Adler).

Parents should try to understand the *intention* of a child's act, which may be a desirable one, though the act itself is undesirable. A mother heard the shrill mewing of kittens from the next room, and called, 'Johnny, what are your doing to the kittens? Be careful not to hurt them!' Johnny replied, 'I am careful. I am carrying them very carefully by their little stems. See!' He appeared in the doorway with a kitten, suspended by its diminutive tail, in each hand.

The future development of a child is harmed more than helped by punishments that humiliate him. It is unwise to say to a child, 'I don't love you, because you disobeyed me.' It is better to say, 'I do not *like* what you did, but of course I love *you.*'

> The structure of world stability and order hath been reared upon, and will continue to be sustained by, the twin pillars of reward and punishment. . . .[15]

> The children who are at the head of their class must receive premiums. They must be encouraged, and when any one of them shows good advancement, for their further development they must be praised and encouraged therein.[16]

Young children should have opportunities for independent investigation, through observation and experimentation. Raw materials with which they can carry on varied creative activities are among the best playthings. Coloured pencils, paints, clay, cartons, tin cans, carboard, wood, materials for making simple musical instruments, can all be used in a variety of ways (see 'The Creative Individual' in chapter 7). Other useful toys are those with which a child can ımitate common adult activities: dolls, small broom and dustpan, toy dishes, cloth, hammer and nails, a toy doctor's or nurse's kit, seeds and small gardening ımplements, etc.

Kindness to animals should be taught in the home; a pet is a great satisfaction to most children. 'Abdu'l-Bahá specifically mentioned the importance of a child's learning to care for an animal.

> Educate the children in their infancy in such a way that they may become exceedingly kind and merciful to the animals. If an animal is sick they should endeavour to cure it; if it is hungry, they should feed it; if it is thirsty, they should satisfy its thirst; if it is tired, they should give it rest.[17]

The education of children in the home is one of the most important of human activities, but this does not mean that parents should be overly serious in their relations with their children. The members of a family should enjoy being together, so that the home is a place of 'joy and delight'. A sense of humour will cause many approaching emotional storms to disappear into laughter.

9

EDUCATION IN SCHOOLS

LEST IT SHOULD be thought that the importance of education for both boys and girls is everywhere recognized, the following information has been taken from a UNESCO report called *Literacy 1969-1971.**

In Africa, around 1970, 63.4% of the adult male population could neither read nor write, but the equivalent percentage for the female population was even worse: 83.7%. In Asia, the figures were 37.0% (men) and 56.7% (women); in the Arab States, 60.5% (men) and 85.7% (women). In the world as a whole, 28.0% of men were illiterate, and 40.3% of women. The world total was nearly *800 million* illiterates (34.3% of the world's adult population), which is more than the world total for 1950 of 700 million (approximately 44% of the adult population at that time).

These statistics show clearly the need for the Bahá'í emphasis on education, and it is noteworthy that in countries lacking an adequate public education Bahá'ís have established their own schools. An early example is the founding of a school for girls by Bahá'ís in

* *Literacy 1969-1971:* Progress achieved in literacy throughout the world (UNESCO, 1972), tables 4 and 5.

Tihrán in 1913, when there was only one other girls' school in the whole city.

The purpose of a school is to provide an environment in which children will learn. This is not the same as stating that 'a school is a place in which teachers teach children'. If the children are not willing to learn, there will be no true education. The teacher is an important part of the school environment, but before discussing the characteristics of a good teacher, we shall mention other aspects of this environment.

School buildings should be well lighted and ventilated, with large rooms so that there is space for a variety of activities, and children can move about freely. Tables and chairs, which can be moved against the wall to provide an open space in the centre of the room, are more useful than the most expensive school desks. Simple wooden kitchen tables and chairs — painted in a variety of colours — are inexpensive, attractive, and useful.

Gay colours should take the place of the dull brown which has so often in the past been used on school walls and woodwork. If necessary, let the children and teachers do the painting. I remember with pleasure a school building where children had decorated the walls with murals and maps. Paintings made by the children, which can be changed frequently, are better wall decorations than sepia prints of 'Old Masters', which adorned the school walls in my childhood. With imagination, ingenuity, and time, a school can be made a beautiful place even when there is little money to spend.

Important equipment for a school includes books, materials for arts and crafts, musical instruments, science materials and equipment. Radio and television are useful, but not as important as raw materials which children can use creatively. When there is little money to spend a library can gradually be built from gifts and second-hand books. In one school at Christmas, children gave new or used books to the library, instad of gifts to the teachers. A craft shop for young children used tin cans, paper plates, waste products from a factory, odds and ends of cloth from a dressmaking establishment, etc. Children made simple musical instruments, and parents and friends loaneu others.

Advanced courses in science usually require expensive equipment, but much elementary science can be done with materials brought from home, or collected nearby. A child who helps to collect or make the things he uses in his work will probably retain what he learns better than the one who is given expensive prepared materials and equipment.

In equipment, as in the decoration of the building, imagination and ingenuity can accomplish miracles.

What Are the Characteristics of a Good Teacher?

1. He (or she) has a sincere liking and respect for children. He values them as human beings, and shows them the same consideration and courtesy that he expects them to show him.

2. He exemplifies in his own life the qualities of character, mind, and spirit that he hopes his pupils will develop.

3. He is emotionally mature, and so does not use children to satisfy his own desire for power over others, or his abnormal need for affection. He does not use them as targets for his fears and angers.

4. He strives to understand the motivations of each individual child, so that he can give the guidance which each one needs. By means of observation, thought, and study he tries to increase his insight into what makes each child behave as he does.

5. He does his best to be scrupulously just. One of the qualities which children value most in teachers is fairness.

6. He has a sense of humour; he knows that a schoolroom without laughter is not only a dull place, but also a poor environment for learning.

7. He likes to learn with the children. He is not afraid to say, 'I don't know the answer to that question, so let us all try to find out.' He knows that it is good for children to realize that there are many things which adults do not know.

8 He is well-informed in the subject-matter he is teaching, and tries to keep up to date with new developments and discoveries.

9. He is familiar with a variety of teaching methods, and is imaginative in devising methods to suit his particular pupils.

10. He believes that he has a responsibility to help

the children's growth in all aspects of their lives — physical, emotional, intellectual, and spiritual — that is, to educate the 'whole child'.

Supervisors and principals have a responsibility to foster the above characteristics in teachers, and should themselves cherish similar values.

> The gentle teacher promoteth the children of the school to the lofty altitude . . .[1]

'How wonderful will it be', 'Abdu'l-Bahá is reported to have said, 'when the teachers are faithful, attracted and assured, educated and refined Bahá'ís, well grounded in the science of pedagogy and familiar with child psychology; thus they may train the children with the fragrances of God. In the scheme of human life the teacher and his system of teaching plays the most important role, carrying with it the heaviest responsibilities and most subtle influence.'[2]

Original Differences in Ability

Children differ in native intelligence as well as in physical health and energy. A class of children of the same chronological age may differ in mental age by as much as six or seven years. It has been my experience, based on individual tests of several hundred children, that a child who makes a high score on an intelligence test will usually show great accomplishment in his school work. But a child who makes a low score may later do excellent work in his studies. His test score did not represent his real ability. He may have been emotionally upset at the time of the test; he may have distrusted his own ability so much that he was unable to make a real effort to answer the questions; he may have been afraid of the test situation or of the examiner. Certainly one should never tell a child or his parents that he is 'dull' or 'stupid'. Even when a child's work is poor, one may hope that whatever is blocking his learning will in time be removed.

Since the amount of intelligence which is actually functioning in each of the children in a class often gives such a wide range in mental age, the teacher must take this into consideration in planning the content of lessons and methods of working. He should vary the amount and complexity of the material, so that each pupil feels confident that he can learn. A child who does poor work in arithmetic may do very well in writing and speaking; praise for the latter may give him courage to work harder to improve the mathematics. A boy's interest in satellites and spaceships may stimulate him to improve his reading, in order to be able to read books in the field that fascinates him. A school which values excellence in many kinds of achievement will provide for individual differences in ability better than one that gives the major emphasis to narrowly academic work.

The prophets also acknowledge this opinion, to wit: That education hath a great effect upon the human race, but they declare that minds and comprehensions are originally different. And this

matter is self-evident; it cannot be refuted. We see
that certain children of the same age, nativity and
race, nay, from the same household, under the
tutorship of one teacher, differ in their minds and
comprehensions. One advanceth rapidly, another is
slow in catching the rays of culture, still another
remaineth in the lowest degree of stupidity.

. . . The calocynth and the thorny cactus can
never by training and development become the
blessed tree. That is to say, training doth not
change the human gem, but it produceth a mar-
velous effect. By this effective power all that is
registered latent of virtues and capacities in the
human reality will be revealed.[3]

No individual should be denied or deprived of
intellectual training although each should receive
according to capacity.[4]

If a pupil is told that his intelligence is less than
his fellow-pupils, it is a very great drawback and
handicap to his progress. He must be encouraged to
advance, by the statement 'You are most capable
and if you endeavour you will attain the highest
degree.'[5]

Methods of Teaching

It is impossible in one chapter to give an adequate
discussion of method. The following are methods
which are mentioned in the Bahá'í Writings, or can be
inferred from them.

1. *The use of discussion* (consultation, conference)
arouses interest and stimulates thinking. Many of the
suggestions made in chapter 12 on Consultation can

be applied to discussion in schools. The following four paragraphs are derived from an earlier book by the author,* and apply directly to discussion in school classes.

An essential part of the planning, conduct, and evaluation of group work is the development of good techniques of discussion. Education in these techniques is begun in the child's first years of school when he is told: 'We all *listen* when Jack is talking'; 'We each wait for our turn'; 'Right now it is Susie's turn to talk; but pretty soon it will be yours.' In the first and second grades, a child begins to learn the responsibilities that go with being a chairman, and the respect which others must show him if the discussion is to be valuable.

By the time third grade representatives attend meetings of the school council they are able to be orderly, helpful group consultants. Meetings of the council and the high-school government, of classes and committees, give training in parliamentary procedure, as a tool for the conduct of discussion. Teachers expect − and usually obtain − orderly procedure in both small and large group conferences. If the group is larger than four or five, each person raises his hand when he wishes to speak and waits to be recognized by the chairman, whether teacher or student. One does not talk to a neighbour in whisper or undertone while a conference is in session. State-

* *Ways toward Self-Discipline:* Genevieve L. Coy (The Dalton School, Inc., 1950), pp. 37-9.

ments should be as clear and concise as the child's level of development makes possible. A considerable amount of conference time is given to helping children improve in accuracy, clarity, and conciseness of statement.

It is evident that the development of really good discussion techniques is a process that must continue over several years. Some children, in their need for attention, will talk too much and not give others a fair share of the time available. Shy children have to be helped to contribute to the group's thinking. Excitement about an idea will result in several children bursting into speech at the same time. A student chairman may need to learn that he must not show favouritism in recognizing members of the group, or that an occasional summary of the preceding discussion will clarify and accelerate the group's work.

The student who has achieved good discussion techniques has learned to discipline himself in a very important area. He has curbed his impulse to burst into speech, in order that the work of the group may move forward efficiently. He has learned to listen with intelligent attention. He gives the ideas of others a fair hearing and can disagree without becoming argumentative or aggressive. Most important of all, perhaps, he may have begun to realize that a group, thinking together, may develop original ideas that no one individual could create by himself.

Many elementary sciences must be made clear to them in the nursery; they must learn them in play, in amusement. Most ideas must be taught them through speech, not by book-learning. One child must question the other concerning these things, and the other child must give the answer. In this way they will make great progress. For example, mathematical problems must also be taught in the form of questions and answers ... Later the children will of their own accord speak with each other concerning these same subjects.[6]

2. *Learning how to investigate independently.* For young children, independent investigation includes learning to observe carefully and to summarize their observations. They may perform simple experiments with seeds, air, water, magnets, etc. As they grow older they can manage more difficult experiments, use several books to supplement their own observations, interview a variety of people, and compare their ideas on a given subject.

Through independent investigation children can be helped to overcome superstition and prejudice. In a third grade a child used the expression 'He was from people of blue blood.' The teacher found that many of the pupils thought that this person's blood was actually blue in colour. She suggested that she prick the finger of each child and that he put a drop of blood on a glass slide. They were astonished to find that no one's blood was blue, and that the colour of a person's skin did not make any difference to the colour of his blood.

3. Schools should provide children with *opportunities to take responsibility* which is appropriate for

their stage of development, to increase their resourcefulness and self-control. They should have experience in making choices and abiding by the results of their decisions.

A good teacher will help children to learn to analyse the probable results of a course of action. He can help them best by the questions he asks them to consider. Some of the children will also contribute questions which help the analysis. Suppose that a sixth grade class have been reading about the life of Buddha, as part of a study of India. It is suggested that they make a play about His life. Questions such as the following are raised: What parts of Buddha's life would be interesting to dramatize? Should we put in the play what He taught the people about how they ought to live? How many boys and girls can we use? Do we want to have costumes? What did people wear in those days? Do we need scenery? What would the costumes and scenery cost? Who would come to the play? Is it useful to take as much time as we would need to make a good play? What would we learn from giving it?

4. Children should form the habit of *evaluating the results of an activity*. This is an important means to the improvement of similar activities. After the play about Buddha has been performed, teacher and class might raise and discuss questions such as these: Which parts of the play were especially well done? Why do you think so? Which parts did not go so well? Why? How could we improve these parts if we gave

the play again? Did the audience enjoy the play? How do we know that they did? What do you think they learned by seeing it? What did we learn?

Curriculum

The Bahá'í Writings do not present a comprehensive course of study for children of different ages, in a given country, at a specific time in history. As aspects of civilization change, details of the curriculum must change. Educators are expected to use intelligence and insight in selecting materials for study which are appropriate to the stage of development mankind has reached, as well as to the interests and needs of a specific group of children.

The Bahá'í Writings do indicate certain general areas of learning which should be included in the curriculum. Among these are the following:

1. *The social studies,* including history, social geography, and principles of human relations. The development of mankind — his inventions, arts, travels, commerce, religion — can be of great interest to children. Guided by their teachers they can learn to understand the ways of living which have resulted in co-operation for human welfare, as well as those which have produced conflict, hatred, and disintegration. As a student grows older he should compare the life of the past with that of the present, and thus be better able to do his part in building a constructive future.

Children of seven and eight years can be helped to understand simple principles of person-to-person relationships. I once asked a group of nine-year-olds to make a list of things a child does which show that he is friendly, and a second list of things which show that he is unfriendly. The lists were then used as a basis for discussing how the group could become more friendly.

Older children can be helped to understand the reasons for the behaviour of a classmate who is generally disliked. They then consider what they can do to help him *want* to act in a more agreeable way. Thus, through the analysis of their everyday experiences, insight into the motivations of human behaviour develops. High-school students who have such an education are ready for a more formal study, which is generally called psychology.

2. *The arts.* A general discussion of the arts and sciences from a Bahá'í viewpoint is given in chapter 7. Here we present references to two specific arts which should be included in the curriculum.

Music

The art of music is divine and effective. It is the food of the soul and spirit. Through the power and charm of music the spirit of man is uplifted.... It is incumbent upon each child to know something of music, for without knowledge of this art, the melodies of instrument and voice cannot be rightly enjoyed.[7]

The language arts

I hope thou wilt acquire great proficiency in writing literature, composition, eloquence of tongue and fluency of speech . . . [8]

Endeavour, so far as it is possible for thee, that day by day thou mayest string the pearls of poesy with sweeter rhythm and more eloquent contents . . . [9]

The Báb subsequently quoted this well-known tradition: 'Treasures lie hidden beneath the throne of God; the key to those treasures is the tongue of poets.'[10]

3. *Sciences.* See the discussion of science in chapter 7.

4. *Preparation for earning a living.* Every Bahá'í should be educated to earn a livelihood. In colleges and universities, this will include courses related to the practice of a specific profession. In the lower schools the development of general character traits needed by people working in any field is an important aspect of education for earning a living; these include responsibility, perseverance, co-operation, and initiative.

5. *Family life and child care.* Secondary school students should be offered a course which will prepare them to fill the responsibilities of family life. Practical experience in working with young children should be provided when at all possible. For example, boys and girls of fifteen or sixteen may spend an hour a day acting as assistants to teachers of kindergarten and

first grade.

6. *Universal language.* In the schools of the future all children will learn a universal language that has been agreed upon by all the countries of the world.

> It behoveth the sovereigns of the world . . . or the ministers of the earth to take counsel together and to adopt one of the existing languages or a new one to be taught to children in schools throughout the world, and likewise one script. Thus the whole earth will come to be regarded as one country. [11]

> We have formerly ordained that people should converse in two languages, yet efforts must be made to reduce them to one, likewise the scripts of the world, that men's lives may not be dissipated and wasted in learning divers languages. Thus the whole earth would come to be regarded as one city and one land. [12]

> Difference of speech is one of the most fruitful causes of dislike and distrust that exists between nations, which are kept apart by their inability to understand each other's language more than by any other reason.
> If everybody could speak one language, how much more easy would it be to serve humanity! [13]

7. *Mathematics* will certainly be included in any course of study, but content and methods of teaching will undoubtedly be modified in relation to the needs of a rapidly-changing scientific and industrial environment.

8. *The great religions.* This should include a study of the lives and teachings of the great Prophets, their

influence on the people of their times, and the present-day status of their religions. Some schools have already included much of this in their curricula. For example, one school presents in sixth grade the lives of Buddha and Krishna, in connection with the history of India and China. In the ninth grade, the teachings of Judaism, Catholicism, and Protestantism are studied, and visits are made to synagogues, cathedrals and churches. A brief study of the life and teachings of Muḥammad is included in the eleventh-grade history course.

The history and teachings of the Bahá'í Faith will necessarily be a most important part of the education of every Bahá'í child.

Since the Bahá'í Faith is dedicated to the development of a new World Order, we may infer that the school curriculum will be selected in relation to the needs of children and society, and not on the basis of what has traditionally been taught. Educators will not be misled by unsubstantiated claims that this or that subject 'trains the mind' or 'improves the reasoning power', or that a certain subject has value just because it is difficult. Selection of subject-matter will be on the basis of what will contribute most to the progress, co-operation, and unity of mankind.

Adult Education

. . . the human perfections are infinite. Thus, however learned a man may be, we can imagine one more learned.[14]

Study the sciences, acquire more and more knowledge. Assuredly one may learn to the end of one's life![15]

... we must not shrink if necessary from beginning our education all over again.[16]

The individual should, prior to engaging in the study of any subject, ask himself what its uses are and what fruit and result will derive from it. If it is a useful branch of knowledge, that is, if society will gain important benefits from it, then he should certainly pursue it with all his heart.[17]

How dull, how uninteresting life must be to an adult who learns almost nothing new! And in a modern civilized country, how difficult it is not to learn! Newspapers, magazines, radio, and television tell of new discoveries in medicine, explorations in Antarctica, the launching of satellites and rockets. Men in the armed services travel to distant countries and return to tell their families of different customs, languages, arts and crafts. Hundreds of inexpensive paperback books compete for the attention of the customer; their titles ranging from *Baby and Child Care* to *The Bull of Minos*. All these media are continually providing adults with an informal education.

Opportunities for more formal adult education are numerous in larger towns and cities. Secondary schools and colleges offer evening courses, as do organizations such as the Young Men's and Young Women's Christian Associations. Summer courses in camps are provided for Boy and Girl Scout leaders. Some cities have reading clinics which adults attend in order to improve their reading speed and comprehension. For people who live on farms and in small villages well-organized correspondence courses send outlines of study and books, in a variety of subjects. Students return their tests and papers to a central office for correction and comment. Libraries publish reading lists for individual or group study.

A group of men and women who are interested in a particular field may organize a study group and, working together without a teacher, increase their knowledge through reading and discussion, or through their participation in an art or craft.

Bahá'ís should be vividly conscious of the need to 'learn to the end of one's life'. They plan and participate in Summer Schools, institutes, and conferences. Local Spiritual Assemblies arrange study courses on a particular book or topic. Individuals who are unable to attend courses give careful study to a Bahá'í book, often using a printed study-outline. Others may do research on a single topic, tracing it through a variety of books. A few who are proficient in two languages may deepen their understanding by translating a pamphlet or book. The true Bahá'í is never satisfied with the present state of his knowledge and insight; he realizes that there will always be new 'perfections' to achieve, and he advances towards them with enthusiasm and joy.

Regard man as a mine rich in gems of inestimable value. Education can, alone, cause it to reveal its treasures, and enable mankind to benefit therefrom.[18]

10

MEN AND WOMEN

In the estimation of God there is no distinction
of sex.[1]

Divine Justice demands that the rights of both
sexes should be equally respected since neither is
superior to the other in the eyes of Heaven.[2]

THESE TWO SHORT statements make clear the Bahá'í
principle of the equality of men and women. Any
man or woman who considers either sex superior to
the other is not abiding by the will of God, and is
committing an injustice. Let men ask themselves such
questions as the following: Do I make sneering
remarks about 'women drivers'? Do I resent the
success of a woman in my own field of work? Do I
really believe that my wife's chief business is to be
my servant? Do I feel that I should make the final
decisions in matters affecting my family? Do I plan to
give my son a better education than my daughter?

Women should ask themselves: Do I expect my
husband to 'put me on a pedestal', to defer to my
whims and fancies? Do I want him to protect me
from all the problems of life, so that I can avoid the
normal responsibilities of a human being? Do I try
to reform him, to make him over into a pattern of my

choice, instead of helping him to develop his own capacities? Do I believe that almost all men are selfish, or liars, or cheats?

Each man (and woman) should analyse his (or her) attitudes and actions to find any hidden evidence of feelings of superiority or inferiority towards the opposite sex, for it is necessary to be fully conscious of such feelings, in order to change them.

The importance of the principle of the equality of the sexes is not limited to life in the home; it has a wider social significance. It is a prerequisite for the tranquillity and happiness of mankind.

> The happiness of mankind will be realized when women and men coordinate and advance equally, for each is the complement and helpmeet of the other.[3]

> Until the reality of equality between man and woman is fully established and attained, the highest social development of mankind is not possible.[4]

> Why should man who is endowed with the sense of justice and sensibilities of conscience be willing that one of the members of the human family should be rated and considered as subordinate? Such differentiation is neither intelligent nor conscientious . . . there must be no difference in the education of male and female, in order that womankind may develop equal capacity and importance with man in the social and economic equation. Then the world will attain unity and harmony.[5]

Men must help women towards a better education and greater freedom to develop their abilities. Wo-

men must do their share; in particular, they should
do their best to profit from increased educational
opportunities. They must avoid thinking of themselves as the weaker sex, and seeking for special privileges on that basis.

> Woman must endeavour then to attain greater
> perfection, to be man's equal in every respect, to
> make progress in all in which she has been backward,
> so that man will be compelled to acknowledge her
> equality of capacity and attainment.[6]

Cultural Conditioning

Some readers of the above discussion may say, 'I
was brought up to believe that men were superior to
women. My mother thought that my father should be
the master, and that her sons were more important
than her daughters.' This attitude towards men and
boys is common to many societies, and it is so in-
grained that it is very difficult to change.

The unconscious learning of attitudes and habits
in early childhood is called by psychologists 'cultural
conditioning'. Parents, neighbours, teachers, all the
institutions of the community, say to the young child,
'This is the *right* way to act, to think, to feel. If you
fail to do this you are not a good (nice, well brought-
up) child.' He learns many of these habits through
imitation of his parents, and feels uncomfortable
when he does not conform.

Neither parents nor children realize that there are
other societies where the proper way to act is just the

opposite of what they are practising. In one society it is wrong to eat shellfish; in another, shellfish are a prized food. In one, the principle of kindness to animals is unknown ('Of course we beat the donkey to make him go faster'); in another, to hurt any animal is a sin.

Standards of good manners also vary markedly from country to country. Some of these forms become meaningless, through repetition, even though consideration for others is the stated justification for them. How many men who stand when a woman enters the room do it because of real respect for her? The rituals used in religious ceremonies have as their purpose to bring the worshipper nearer to God. How often does the form become a mechanical repetition, with no spiritual content? Yet the individual feels that he would be 'sinning' if he did not do what he had been taught from his earliest years.

One of the most important examples of cultural conditioning is found in attitudes towards competition. Not all societies are competitive, and there is much evidence to indicate that the desire to compete for money, position, etc., is not an inborn (inherited) characteristic. Yet a large majority of people in North America and Europe act on the assumption that all men are naturally competitive, and that this trait can never be eradicated from human nature. As a result we suffer from wars of conquest, extremes of poverty and wealth, defamation of the characters of innocent citizens, and a host of other evils. (A valuable brief discussion of co-operation versus competition is given in Ashley Montagu's book, *On Being Human*.)

One of the best ways to realize how much of our behaviour is a result of cultural conditioning is to read descriptions of the customs of other societies in books such as *Patterns of Culture* and *The Chrysanthemum and the Sword*, by Ruth Benedict, or *Growing Up in New Guinea* and *Coming of Age in Samoa*, by Margaret Mead. Books such as these are extremely interesting, and give us an understanding of people whose way of life is very different from our own.

It is also valuable for each of us to make a list of our own habits which we think of as 'second nature'. Many of these have no good reason now, although they may have had in the past. In practice it is usually better to continue conforming to convention (though not in cases where others are harmed, or where the activity takes too much time). But if we realize how much of our own habitual behaviour has little *reason* behind it, perhaps we will be less likely to look down on people from other cultures whose customs are different from ours.

It should be clear from the above discussion that culturally conditioned habits of behaviour are learned. What has been learned can be unlearned; another response, another habit, can be substituted. Therefore men and women who have been conditioned to feel that it is right and proper for one sex to be superior to the other, can change. It is not easy for most people to do this, but those who become

Bahá'ís must make a persistent effort to do so. Divine justice requires that they do. We must not take the attitude of an elderly Muslim who, when he became a Bahá'í and learned of the principle of the equality of the sexes, said, 'Since our Lord Bahá'u'lláh said men and women are equal, it must be true. But I hope I don't live to see the day when it is put into practice!'

Marriage

In a true Bahá'í marriage the two parties must become fully united both spiritually and physically, so that they may attain eternal union throughout all the worlds of God, and improve the spiritual life of each other. This is Bahá'í matrimony.[7]

A. Engagement

If the intention in marriage is to begin a relationship which will continue throughout eternity, the engagement cannot be entered into lightly or on impulse. The love of the two for one another must be so deep that 'It is as though from all eternity God had kneaded the very essence of their beings for the love of one another.' Each must become well informed of the character of the other, and both must consider thoughtfully and prayerfully whether they can be patient with each other's faults. Both must centre their hearts in love for God, and dedicate their lives to following His teachings.

... the tie between them is none other than the Word of God. ... Thus the husband and wife are brought into affinity, are united and harmonized, even as though they were one person. Through their mutual union, companionship and love great results are produced in the world, both material and spiritual. The spiritual result is the appearance of divine bounties. The material result is the children who are born in the cradle of the love of God, who are nurtured by the breast of the knowledge of God. . .[8]

The behaviour and attitudes which are essential in a true Bahá'í marriage are stated so clearly and beautifully in the following words attributed to 'Abdu'l-Bahá that we quote them in full. They are used by Bahá'ís, although they do not have the status of authenticated Scripture.

'The bond that unites hearts most perfectly is loyalty. True lovers once united must show forth the utmost faithfulness one to another. You must dedicate your knowledge, your talents, your fortunes, your titles, your bodies and your spirits to God, to Bahá'u'lláh and to each other. Let your hearts be spacious, as spacious as the universe of God!

'Allow no trace of jealousy to creep between you, for jealousy, like unto poison, vitiates the very essence of love. Let not the ephemeral incidents and accidents of this changeful life cause a rift between you. When differences present themselves, take counsel together in secret, lest others magnify a speck into a mountain.

Harbour not in your hearts any grievance, but rather explain its nature to each other with such frankness and understanding that it will disappear, leaving no remembrance. Choose fellowship and amity and turn away from jealousy and hypocrisy.

'Your thoughts must be lofty, your ideals luminous, your minds spiritual, so that your souls may become a dawning-place for the Sun of Reality. Let your hearts be like unto two pure mirrors reflecting the stars of the heaven of love and beauty.

'Together make mention of noble aspirations and heavenly concepts. Let there be no secrets one from another. Make your home a haven of rest and peace. Be hospitable, and let the doors of your house be open to the faces of friends and strangers. Welcome every guest with radiant grace and let each feel that it is his own home.

'No mortal can conceive the union and harmony which God has designed for man and wife. Nourish continually the tree of your union with love and affection, so that it will remain ever green and verdant throughout all seasons and bring forth luscious fruits for the healing of nations.

'O beloved of God, may your home be a vision of the paradise of Abhá, so that whosoever enters there may feel the essence of purity and harmony, and cry out from the heart: "Here is the home of love! Here is the palace of love! Here is the nest of love! Here is the garden of love!"

'Be like two sweet-singing birds perched upon the

highest branches of the tree of life, filling the air with songs of love and rapture.

'Lay the foundation of your affection in the very centre of your spiritual being, at the very heart of your consciousness, and let it not be shaken by adverse winds.

'And when God gives you sweet and lovely children, consecrate yourselves to their instruction and guidance so that they may become imperishable flowers of the divine rose-garden, nightingales of the ideal paradise, servants of the world of humanity, and the fruit of the tree of your life.

'Live in such harmony that others may take your lives for an example and may say one to another: "Look how they live like two doves in one nest, in perfect love, affinity and union. It is as though from all eternity God had kneaded the very essence of their beings for the love of one another."

'Attain the ideal love that God has destined for you, so that you may become partakers of eternal life forthwith. Quaff deeply from the fountain of truth, and dwell all the days of your life in a paradise of glory, gathering immortal flowers from the garden of divine mysteries.

'Be to each other as heavenly lovers and divine beloved ones dwelling in a paradise of love. Build your nest on the leafy branches of the tree of love. Soar into the clear atmosphere of love. Sail upon the shoreless sea of love. Walk in the eternal rose-garden of love. Bathe in the shining rays of the sun of love.

Be firm and steadfast in the path of love. Perfume your nostrils with the fragrance from the flowers of love. Attune your ears to the soul-entrancing melodies of love. Let your aims be as generous as the banquets of love, and your words as a string of white pearls from the ocean of love. Drink deeply of the elixir of love, so that you may live continually in the reality of Divine Love.'[9]

A man and woman who are contemplating marriage may well read and consider together each paragraph of this advice. Then let them decide whether they are ready to devote themselves − body, mind, heart, and spirit − to so high an undertaking.

B. Consent

In many parts of the world it has been customary for parents to select a wife for a son, and the young couple have had little voice in the matter. Bahá'ís, no matter in what country they live, do not follow this custom. The man and woman must become well acquainted with each other and make their own decision as to whether they love and understand each other enough to marry. When the choice has been made all living parents must consent to the marriage before the couple may be united in a Bahá'í ceremony.

One purpose of requiring the consent of the parents is to delay (or prevent) a marriage which seems to them ill-advised, or based on a temporary attraction. Another purpose is to maintain harmony between the two families which are brought into close relationship by the marriage of a daughter of one family to the son of another.

As We desired to bring about love and friendship and the unity of the people, therefore We made it [marriage] conditional upon the consent of the parents also, that enmity and ill-feeling might be avoided.[10]

In considering whether to give consent to a marriage, parents who are true Bahá'ís will consider the welfare and happiness of the son and daughter, rather than their own comfort and happiness. They will not be influenced by such factors as whether the marriage will contribute to their own social or financial position, whether they will enjoy association with the son-in-law or the daughter-in-law, or whether the young man's work will necessitate his taking a well-loved daughter far from her father and mother. The parents must endeavour to be completely unselfish and just in coming to a decision.

As to the question of marriage, according to the law of God: First you must select one, and then it depends upon the consent of the father and mother. Before your selection they have no right of interference.[11]

This eternal bond should be made secure by a firm covenant, and the intention should be to foster harmony, fellowship and unity and to attain everlasting life . . .[12]

C. The ceremony

In some countries of the world the local Bahá'í Spiritual Assembly is permitted to perform a legal marriage ceremony. But in the majority of places where Bahá'ís reside this is not yet possible, and a young man and woman must have a civil marriage to meet the legal requirements. While it is essential to meet the legal requirements of the country in which they live, to Bahá'ís the true marriage ceremony is of course that ordained by Bahá'u'lláh, in which the man and woman dedicate their lives to God and to one another. In the presence of witnesses each declares, 'We will all, verily, abide by the will of God.' The remainder of the ceremony may include music, prayers, and other readings from Scripture, chosen by the bride and bridegroom to accord with their personal preferences.

D. Divorce

The Bahá'í teachings with respect to divorce are summarized in the following statement by 'Abdu'l-Bahá.

The friends must strictly refrain from divorce unless something arises which compels them to separate because of their aversion for each other; in that case, with the knowledge of the Spiritual Assembly, they may decide to separate. They must then be patient and wait one complete year. If during this year harmony is not re-established between them, then their divorce may be realized. ... The foundation of the Kingdom of God is

based upon harmony and love, oneness, relationship and union, not upon differences, especially
between husband and wife.[13]

In seeking a divorce, Bahá'ís will necessarily
conform to the laws of the country in which they
live. But if a Bahá'í couple enter into marriage thoughtfully and prayerfully, with the intention of building
a relationship that will continue throughout eternity,
divorce should very seldom be necessary.

*   *   *

'Glory be unto Thee, O my God! Verily this
Thy servant and this Thy maidservant have
gathered under the shadow of Thy mercy and
they are united through Thy favour and generosity. O Lord! Assist them in this Thy world
and Thy kingdom and destine for them every
good through Thy bounty and grace. O Lord!
Confirm them in Thy servitude and assist them
in Thy service. Suffer them to become the signs
of Thy Name in Thy world and protect them
through Thy bestowals which are inexhaustible
in this world and the world to come. O Lord!
They are supplicating the kingdom of Thy merci-
fulness and invoking the realm of Thy singleness.
Verily, they are married in obedience to Thy
command. Cause them to become the signs of
harmony and unity until the end of time.

'Verily, Thou art the Omnipotent, the Omni-
present and the Almighty.'

'Abdu'l-Bahá

11

FAIRNESS TO YOURSELF AND OTHERS

BAHÁ'ÍS SOMETIMES SAY that an individual cannot administer justice, that this can be done only by a group such as a Spiritual Assembly. It is true that such a group, animated by Bahá'í principles, will usually give a wiser decision on any problem or conflict than can even the wisest individual member working alone. However, everyone in his daily life meets dozens of situations in which his response might be fair or unfair, just or unjust. Were this not true Bahá'u'lláh would surely not have written the following:

> Be fair to yourselves and to others, that the evidences of justice may be revealed, through your deeds, among Our faithful servants.[1]

This chapter, then, deals primarily with the meaning of fairness in the life of the individual. Many of the earlier chapters have touched on various aspects of this topic. Here we recapitulate some of these points and add other illustrations.

What Does Justice Require?

The person who strives to be fair is not influenced in his decisions by his own likes and dislikes, by what he wants or does not want, by envy or jealousy.

The second attribute of perfection is justice and impartiality. This means to have no regard for one's own personal benefits and selfish advantages ... It means to consider the welfare of the community as one's own.[2]

The just man or woman gathers all the available facts and as much background information as possible. He avoids hearsay evidence, knowing that it is often untrustworthy.

O Son of Spirit! The best beloved of all things in My sight is Justice; turn not away therefrom if thou desirest Me, and neglect it not that I may confide in thee. By its aid thou shalt see with thine own eyes and not through the eyes of others, and shalt know of thine own knowledge and not through the knowledge of they neighbour ....[3]

The fair person weighs all the information thoughtfully, carefully, without prejudice. He does not make impulsive decisions, or extreme judgements.

Whoso cleaveth to justice, can, under no circumstances, transgress the limits of moderation.[4]

The fair individual is fully conscious of the motives, both material and spiritual, which determine his decisions. If a teacher reprimands a student he should know whether he does so because of anger, hurt pride, or because he honestly thinks it essential to the student's development.

Two sections in chapter 5, 'Some Errors in the Use of Intelligence' and 'The Use of Intelligence in Making

Choices', analyse aspects of fairness, and a re-reading of these pages is suggested.

Be Fair to Yourself

What does it mean to be fair to yourself? The following are some of the ways in which such fairness is shown.

1. *Use opportunities to learn, to improve.* Do not let inertia, inflexibility, or prejudice deprive you of fine new ideas and experiences. Do not be scornful of new inventions and discoveries. Investigate to find out what valuable materials and ideas have resulted from recent experimentation.

When you first heard of the Bahá'í Faith, did you say to yourself, 'I will study this to find out what is good in these teachings', or did you think, 'This sounds like an attack on true religion. I will do my best to keep my friends from having anything to do with it'? If your reaction was the latter, was it caused by inertia, an unwillingness to make the effort to investigate? Or was it due to inflexibility; had your ideas and feelings about religion become set in a mould which you feared to break? Or were you prejudiced against any religious teaching which was different from the faith of your early childhood?

2. *Protecting your health* is another way of being fair to yourself. If, without a good reason, you sleep too little, or eat an unbalanced diet, or smoke a great deal, you are running the danger of injuring your

health, and so decreasing your usefulness and happiness.

3. *If you habitually take on more work than you can do well,* you are being unfair to yourself; and often you are being unfair to others, who should be doing the work you have unwisely agreed to do. If at times it seems really necessary for you to undertake the jobs of two people, do the most important things first, and do not feel guilty about the jobs you had to leave undone.

People sometimes undertake too much because of a mistaken ideal of perfection. If a man insists on doing one job *perfectly,* it often means that he has to neglect more important work. If a woman is ironing a dress and feels that she must not leave one tiny crease in it, she may not have time to prepare a wholesome and appetizing lunch for her children. Which is more important? The person who is fair to himself uses good judgement in choosing the work on which he will spend his time and energy.

4. *Honesty with yourself* is another indication of fairness. This includes readiness to acknowledge your own mistakes. It is unfair to yourself, as well as to others, to blame someone else, or something in the environment, for the undesirable results of your own actions.

Occasionally a person unconsciously 'acts a part'; he tries to be something other than he really is. His motives may be excellent, although frequently the act is a way of strengthening his own ego. Psychologists say that such a person is building up a 'persona'; that is, he is putting on a mask like those once worn in a play by the *dramatis personae*. An individual with a persona often gives the impression that he is not being himself; but it would probably not be fair to accuse him of insincerity, since he does not realize what he is doing.

To act a part which is foreign to your real self, consciously or unconsciously, is to be unfair to yourself and to waste time and energy.

Be Fair to Others

If thou lookest toward justice, choose thou for others what thou choosest for thyself.[5]

Lay not on any soul a load which ye would not wish to be laid upon you, and desire not for any one the things ye would not desire for yourselves.[6]

He that is unjust in his judgment is destitute of the characteristics that distinguish man's station.[7]

Much of chapter 2 deals with ways in which we may be unfair to others. Here we present further illustrations of lack of fairness.

1. *To take credit for the ideas or work of another is unfair.* Often this is done without intent to deceive, but is due to carelessness. I hear an original thought expressed by a friend; a little later I use the idea in conversation, giving credit to my friend. Then I use it again, and fail to say that it was not my own idea.

In Bahá'í group work, in a Spiritual Assembly for example, ideas are put into a common pool by various members. It is understood that these ideas become the property of the group who use them to help solve a problem. This is a very different procedure from that in which an individual takes and uses the ideas of another, without giving credit to the source.

Bahá'í publications occasionally print an article without giving any indication of the author. Committee reports, whether or not signed by the secretary, may be assumed to be the work of the whole committee. The same is of course true of reports by Local and National Assemblies. But other articles should, in fairness to both the author and the reader, be signed by the writer. On one occasion a Bahá'í was asked by a committee to write a statement on the conduct of Workshops, based on his own comprehensive experience. He spent a great deal of time and thought in writing the article. Later the committee published it in the bulletin, but gave no credit to the author. This deprived the readers of knowledge of the kind of experience on which the article was based. While the writer was not really upset by this failure to give recognition to his work, he was astonished at the committee's action.

2. The person who is fair to others does not borrow and then *fail to return what he has borrowed.* Do you have empty spaces on your bookshelves that should be filled with the books your acquaintances

have forgotten to return? Can you imagine *why* they have been so unfair to you?

3. It is unfair to others *to avoid work which is your proper job,* and to scheme so that others will have to do it. Is your sudden headache a real one, or is it an excuse for avoiding a distasteful task?

4. It is unjust *to make unnecessary work for others.* I have observed two households, in each of which a young man of college age often rises quite late when he is home on vacation. In each home a maid cooks, cleans, and does the laundry. One young man goes to the kitchen when he wakes at 10.30 or later, and quietly prepares his own breakfast. In the other home the 18-year-old rises at 11.00, and tells the maid that he would like breakfast at 11.30. Then later he goes to the kitchen and says, 'Now I am ready for lunch.' He seems completely unaware of being unfair to the maid. Both these young men consider themselves devoted Bahá'ís.

5. It is unfair *for an employee to take advantage of any special relationship he may have with his employer,* by doing less work than he is expected to do. If the employer is a relative, it is unfair for the worker habitually to leave work half an hour early. If one Bahá'í works for another Bahá'í he should be extremely careful not to impose on the relationship by such actions as taking a two-hour lunch break when he is supposed to have only one hour.

6. Is it fair for one person *to use the home of a friend as a hotel,* coming and going with little or no

warning to his host or hostess? In countries such as the United States and Canada, where telephones are usually available, there seems little excuse for a Bahá'í who comes to a friend's house and announces that he is going to spend the night, unless he has enquired by phone whether this is convenient. What can we say of the courtesy of a person who frequently appears just at meal time, sometimes accompanied by four or five others? And he obviously expects that the hostess will be a kind of short-order magician, making the food she had planned for the family of five serve ten bountifully!

In some parts of the world, where hotels are infrequent and Bahá'ís often have very little money, it is customary to spend nights on a long trip in the homes of other Bahá'ís. This is one way in which pioneers exchange news and are refreshed by seeing their friends. But it is only in an emergency that a traveller will appear at a Bahá'í home without giving notice of his coming.

> ... No man should enter the house of his friend save at his friend's pleasure, nor lay hands upon his treasures nor prefer his own will to his friend's, and in no wise seek an advantage over him.[8]

The Concept of Equality in the Bahá'í Faith

A Bahá'í's understanding of the concept of equality is an essential part of his application of ideals of fairness and justice. In the sight of God all men are equal.

'Abdu'l-Bahá states this clearly and definitely, as follows:

> In the estimation of God all men are equal; there is no distinction or preferment for any soul in the dominion of His justice and equity.[9]

The Bahá'í teachings state that all men should be equal before the law.

> Justice is not limited, it is a universal quality. Its operation must be carried out in all classes, from the highest to the lowest.[10]

> ... prince, peer and peasant alike have equal rights to just treatment, there must be no favour shown to individuals.[11]

> All men are equal before the law, which must reign absolutely.[12]

A wealthy or prominent man who commits a crime must not be punished less severely than a poor or obscure man who is guilty of the same crime. No one should be able to resort to bribery to gain exemption from an onerous duty. Wherever men are not equal before the law, disunity and conflict will certainly result.

The Bahá'í concept of equality does not, of course, imply that all men and women are equal in education, in skill, in achievement. In these there are degrees, but the one with more education or greater skill must not be thought to be superior as a human being, as a creation of God.

The lovers of mankind, these are the superior men, of whatever nation, creed, or colour they may be.[13]

In most undertakings it is necessary to delegate various responsibilities, and, ideally, each does the kind of work for which he is best fitted. In a hospital doctors, technicians, nurses, and orderlies are needed, as well as supervisors who see that all the staff work together efficiently and harmoniously. In any organization such differences in types of work are necessary. Each worker is an essential part of the functioning of the whole, and should feel pride and satisfaction in his service to any enterprise which is for the welfare of mankind. Unfortunately competitive societies often fail to recognize the importance of the contribution made by the so-called humble worker, even though the efficiency of the economy would be destroyed if he did not do his work. Lacking such recognition at the present time, the individual worker must obtain his satisfaction from his earnings, and from knowing that his work is a useful contribution to our common life.

One of Bahá'u'lláh's teachings is the adjustment of means of livelihood in human society. Under this adjustment there can be no extremes in human conditions as regards wealth and sustenance. For the community needs financier, farmer, merchant and labourer just as an army must be composed of commander, officers and privates. . . . Each in his station in the social fabric must be competent;

each in his function according to ability; but justness of opportunity for all.[14]

This chapter has shown that fairness to oneself requires a flexible attitude towards experience, a willingness to investigate new ideas, honesty, and the ability to discipline one's immediate desires in order to achieve future goals. Fairness to others demands that one have 'no regard for one's own . . . selfish advantages'; it requires an effort to enter imaginatively into the heart and mind of another, so that one has some understanding of his desires and needs. It is dependent on the conviction that, since 'In the estimation of God all men are equal', we must avoid attitudes of superiority or inferiority which separate us from others.

There is no force on earth that can equal in its conquering power the force of justice and wisdom. . . . There can be no doubt whatever that if the day star of justice, which the clouds of tyranny have obscured, were to shed its light upon men, the face of the earth would be completely transformed.[15]

12

CONSULTATION

MANY GROUPS — social, educational, scientific, political, religious — carry on their work by means of conferences. They share their ideas and plans, and come to a decision by voting.

The essential characteristic of Bahá'í consultation is that the consultants are in spiritual unity, even when their ideas differ to a marked degree. Ideally, the members of the group function as 'one soul in different bodies'. They gladly share their experiences and ideas; they are willing to become merged in the thinking of the group. The self-centred person is unable to do this; he is sure his ideas are right, and feels that he must compel others to agree with him. He may hear what the others say, but he does not really try to understand their meaning. Before he can become a useful consultant he must re-educate himself until he is able to think in terms of 'we', rather than 'I'.

> The heaven of divine wisdom is illumined with the two luminaries of consultation and compassion. . .[1]

> . . . true consultation is spiritual conference in the attitude and atmosphere of love.[2]

'They must then proceed with the utmost devotion, courtesy, dignity, care and moderation to express their views. They must in every matter search out the truth and not insist upon their own opinion, for stubbornness and persistence in one's views will lead ultimately to discord and wrangling and the truth will remain hidden. The honoured members must with all freedom express their own thoughts, and it is in no wise permissible for one to belittle the thought of another, nay, he must with moderation set forth the truth, and should differences of opinion arise a majority of voices must prevail, and all must obey and submit to the majority. . . . In short, whatsoever thing is arranged in harmony and with love and purity of motive, its result is light, and should the least trace of estrangement prevail the result shall be darkness upon darkness.'[3]

Bahá'ís consult in Local and National Spiritual Assemblies, in committees, in various conferences, at Nineteen Day Feasts, and at summer schools. Whenever they come together to plan how to achieve a Bahá'í goal, the principles of consultation should be applied. In 'spiritual conference' The Bahá'í has an opportunity and an obligation to put into practice the suggestions made in earlier chapters of this book.

An atmosphere of fellowship, kindness, and love is the first essential in consultation. But this atmosphere may be present and still the consultation may be less effective than it should be. In what way is the necessary freedom of expression to be achieved? Can anything be done to help the person who seems to have good ideas, but is almost inarticulate in stating them?

The following suggestions have been developed through the experience of both Bahá'ís and non-Bahá'ís; they are applicable to the work of professional and social welfare groups, as well as to the consultation of Bahá'í Assemblies and committees.

Suggestions for Chairmen

1. The attitude of committee members should be that of learning together. The chairman should do all that he can to foster this attitude.

2. The agenda of a meeting should be sent to members several days before the meeting. When this is not possible, the agenda should be given to each person or read aloud at the beginning of the meeting. Members should be given an opportunity to add to the agenda.

3. The chairman should think through the material for the meeting as imaginatively as possible. Think of ways in which these ideas may be stated as questions, to stimulate the thinking of the group, if this is needed.

4. Try to get agreement on procedures. Sometimes it is useful to give out a list of suggested procedures and ask the group to agree to apply the ones which they think are most useful.

5. Convey enthusiasm and good humour! Even when you are feeling discouraged about the progress of the work, the other members do not need to know you are feeling that way. In case the consultation has

been very disorganized, it may be necessary for the chairman to speak of the time that has been wasted, but do not scold!

6. If you know that a few people have ideas which have not come out in the discussion, ask questions that will give them a chance to state their particular concerns.

7. A wandering, confused statement often has in it the germ of a good idea. The chairman can pick this up, restate it clearly, and ask for discussion on it.

8. While the chairman should be as tactful as possible, committee meetings should not be used as therapy for the emotional problems of an individual. For example, the compulsive talker sometimes has to be stopped.

9. Summarize at strategic points and fairly frequently. This tends to help the group feel that they are making progress. It helps keep a thread of continuity in the discussion, or it shows how scattered and irrelevant the comments have been.

10. The chairman has the responsibility of making sure that members do not feel that a decision is pushed through without adequate consultation: in other words, that it has been 'railroaded'.

Parliamentary procedure should have for its object the attainment of the light of truth upon questions presented and not furnish a battle ground for opposition and self-opinion. Antagonism and contradiction are unfortunate and always destructive to truth. . . .

... consultation must have for its object the investigation of truth. He who expresses an opinion should not voice it as correct and right but set it forth as a contribution to the consensus of opinion; for the light of reality becomes apparent when two opinions coincide. A spark is produced when flint and steel come together. Man should weigh his opinions with the utmost serenity, calmness and composure. Before expressing his own views he should carefully consider the views already advanced by others. If he finds that a previously expressed opinion is more true and worthy, he should accept it immediately and not wilfully hold to an opinion of his own. By this excellent method he endeavours to arrive at unity and truth.[4]

Suggestions for Members of Consulting Groups

1. Over the course of one or two meetings consultation should be rather evenly distributed among all the members. The one who frequently talks more than his share is depriving others. The one who takes little part in discussion is failing to take his share of responsibility.

In all matters moderation is desirable. If a thing is carried to excess, it will prove a source of evil.[5]

2. Even the most carefully chosen words sometimes fail to convey the speaker's attitude. We should try to respond to the speaker's *intention*, even though his words may be inadequate or tactless.

3. Those who tend to get impatient need to

practise patience. But a member who frequently evokes impatience in others needs to analyse his own conduct to try to discover why he has that effect, and then do something about it!

4. We need to use imagination in entering into the mind and heart of others. To say, 'I can't understand why he feels that way . . . *I* wouldn't!' shows lack of imagination, and failure to realize how greatly individuals differ.

5. Make your first sentence count! Avoid, 'Of course I know most of you will not agree with me', or, 'As I was walking down the street the other day — it must have been last Friday on my way to the Post Office . . . no, I guess it was to buy groceries — it suddenly occurred to me that . . .' Avoid all similar unproductive remarks.

6. When you have clearly stated an idea, *stop talking*. Many good ideas fail because the speaker repeats and repeats, and the idea is lost in the flood of words. Other members can ask questions if they need more information. Also, continued repetition sometimes gives the impression that the speaker is trying to force the other members to agree with him.

7. If there is a short period of silence it often means that the members are doing some good thinking. It is not necessary to say just anything in order to fill the silence with words.

8. When a member is presenting an idea, let him finish his statement before you interrupt with questions or opinions. His next sentence may answer the

question you had in mind.

9. In groups as large as perhaps five or more, a member should raise his hand when he wishes to speak, and then wait to be recognized by the chairman. This helps to avoid interruption of a speaker, or delays between speeches when people are trying not to interrupt. To wave one's hand wildly while another person is speaking is inexcusable.

10. Disagreement with ideas is often necessary. But no one has to be a whining complainer!

> 'In this day, assemblies of consultation are of the greatest importance and a vital necessity. . . . The members thereof must take counsel together in such wise that no occasion for ill-feeling or discord may arise. This can be attained when every member expresseth with absolute freedom his own opinion and setteth forth his argument. Should any one oppose, he must on no account feel hurt for not until matters are fully discussed can the right way be revealed. The shining spark of truth cometh forth only after the clash of differing opinions.'[6]

The following suggestions apply more directly to the meetings of Bahá'í Assemblies and committees. Some of them will not be needed when all the members are mature Bahá'ís; they are included for the help of those who have not yet understood the full implications of Bahá'í love and fellowship.

1. Even to think that 'James is not a truly spiritual person, or he would not have voted that way', is destructive of unity. Let us all act on the conviction that

every member is trying to serve the Faith to the very best of his ability.

2. Disagreement with a member's ideas does not show lack of respect for him, nor doubt of his devotion to the Faith.

3. To scold another member for something he has said or done is seldom useful. If he has made a mistake he probably feels more unhappy about it than anyone else does. Attention should be on future action, not on past errors.

4. Whenever possible we should state the Bahá'í principles which apply to a problem. When there has been lengthy discussion of a question, the chairman, or another member, should sum up the principles involved before the vote is taken.

5. Each member should avoid trying to advance his point of view by quoting Bahá'u'lláh, 'Abdu'l-Bahá, or Shoghi Effendi incorrectly, or out of context, in a way which fails to present the true intention of the author. A member who uses quotations in this way is probably not conscious of his error, but is carried away by the conviction that his solution is the right one. Other members should know the teachings so well that they are not misled by such inaccurate or incomplete quotations. Occasionally the Assembly may need to ask for the exact source (book and page) of a quotation. The use of pilgrims' notes as a source of authority for an action should never be permitted.

6. The chairman should exercise the prerogative

of limiting discussion when necessary. Members can help the chairman to bring a too-lengthy discussion to an end by making a motion to put the question to the vote. Such a motion can always be voted down if the majority wish to continue the discussion.

7. The most important questions should be brought up relatively early in the meeting.

8. No member has a right to insist on speaking after the Assembly has voted to adjourn.

9. When a committee (or an individual) presents a matter to the Assembly, the members should listen with close attention and ask any questions that may be needed to clarify or amplify the ideas presented. They should *not* express approval or disapproval while the committee members are meeting with them. *After* consultation the Assembly should come to a decision, and then convey this to the committee.

10. When an Assembly is consulting on a question, vigorous differences of opinion are often desirable. But when a vote has been taken, all members must accept the decision of the majority, and this acceptance should be whole-hearted and gracious.

11. We should frequently evaluate our consultations. In what ways have we improved? What are now our greatest weaknesses? Which of these should we work on next?

In discussions look toward the reality without being self-opinionated. Let no one assert and insist upon his own mere opinion; nay, rather, let each investigate the reality with the greatest love and fellowship. Consult upon every matter and when one presents the point of view of the reality itself, that shall be acceptable to all.[7]

To a group of American Bahá'ís who visited 'Abdu'l-Bahá in 1898 He is reported to have said, 'Great mercy and blessings are promised to the people of your land, but on one condition: that their hearts are filled with the fire of love, that they live in perfect kindness and harmony like one soul in different bodies, like one soul in different bodies.' When this ideal is attained in the meetings of an Assembly or committee the decisions will be kind, wise, and just. The members will return to their homes with renewed strength and devotion, and with a deeper understanding of the meaning of Bahá'í fellowship and unity.

* * *

'O my God! O my God! Unite the hearts of Thy servants, and reveal to them Thy great purpose. May they follow Thy commandments and abide in Thy law. Help them, O God, in their endeavour, and grant them strength to serve Thee. O God! Leave them not to themselves, but guide their steps by the light of Thy knowledge and cheer their hearts by Thy love. Verily, Thou art their Helper and their Lord.'

Bahá'u'lláh

13

JOY GIVES US WINGS

IN *The Oriental Rose,* Mary Hanford Ford tells the story of Mrs. C. who was a guest of 'Abdu'l-Bahá in Haifa. She was much depressed by the feeling of her own unworthiness, and continually took herself to task for her faults. 'Abdu'l-Bahá frequently said to her, 'Be happy!' and she began to wonder why He seemed to address her in this way more often than He did others. Finally she enquired why He urged her to be happy. He replied, 'I tell you to be happy because we cannot know the spiritual life unless we are happy.' Then Mrs. C. exclaimed, 'But tell me, what is the spiritual life? I have heard ever since I was born about the spiritual life, and no one could ever explain to me what it is!' 'Abdu'l-Bahá said, 'Characterize thyself with the characteristics of God, and thou shalt know the spiritual life!'

Mrs C. began to query, 'What did he mean? What are the characteristics of God? They must be the great attributes, of course, Love, Beauty, Generosity, Justice,' and so on in beautiful succession.

All day long her mind was flooded with the divine puzzle, and all day long she was happy. She did not give a thought to her duties, and yet when she arrived at the moment of her evening's reckoning, she could not remember that she had left them undone.

At last she began to understand. If she was absorbed in Heavenly ideals, they would translate themselves into deeds necessarily, and her days and nights would be full of light.[1]

In *The Hidden Words,* Bahá'u'lláh commands us to rejoice.

O Son of Man! Rejoice in the gladness of thine heart, that thou mayest be worthy to meet Me and to mirror forth My beauty.[2]

'Abdu'l-Bahá had this to say of His own happiness in prison:

I myself was in prison forty years — one year alone would have been impossible to bear — nobody survived that imprisonment more than a year! But, thank God, during all those forty years I was supremely happy! Every day, on waking, it was like hearing good tidings, and every night infinite joy was mine. Spirituality was my comfort, and turning to God was my greatest joy.[3]

Does the command to be joyful, to be happy, mean that we need experience no problems, tests, and griefs? Certainly not. It does mean that when our hearts are filled with the love of God and the desire to serve Him, we will face our difficulties joyfully.

Joy gives us wings! In times of joy our strength is more vital, our intellect keener, and our understanding less clouded. We seem better able to cope

with the world and to find our sphere of usefulness. But when sadness visits us we become weak,
our strength leaves us, our comprehension is dim
and our intelligence veiled. The actualities of life
seem to elude our grasp, the eyes of our spirits fail
to discover the sacred mysteries, and we become
even as dead beings.

There is no human being untouched by these
two influences; but all the sorrow and the grief
that exist come from the world of matter — the
spiritual world bestows only the joy!

. . . the spiritual Kingdom never causes sadness.
A man living with his thoughts in this Kingdom
knows perpetual joy. The ills all flesh is heir to do
not pass him by, but they only touch the surface
of his life, the depths are calm and serene.[4]

You must live in the utmost happiness. If any
trouble or vicissitude comes into your lives, if your
heart is depressed on account of health, livelihood
or vocation, let not these things affect you. They
should not cause unhappiness, for Bahá'u'lláh has
brought you divine happiness.[5]

Let us consider some of the experiences which the
true Bahá'í should meet with spiritual joy and tran-
quility.

Tests and Trials

The word 'test' is used frequently in the Bahá'í
Writings. Some of these tests, or trials, are the consequences of a person's own actions. He makes a mistake
and has to suffer the consequences; he is unkind, and
makes a friend unhappy; he fails to pay his debts, and

becomes known as untrustworthy. It is only when he analyses his behaviour, and realizes his errors, that he will make an effort to change his conduct. If he does not see his mistakes and try to improve, he has failed to meet the 'test' he has given himself.

Other tests and trials are sent to us by God for our development and perfecting. Some people have difficulty in accepting this idea; they even feel that God is unjust when he presents us with problems. But this is just what a good teacher does in order to educate his pupils. He gives them problems to solve, and tests to take, which are within their ability if they work to the top limit of their capacity. If he makes the tests too easy the good student will feel that his teacher is not interested in him, or underestimates his ability!

Since God is omniscient, He adjusts each individual's tests to his capacity. We should realize that when a trial or problem seems impossibly difficult, it is because we are not working at it with all our might, and with full dependence on God's help.

He will never deal unjustly with any one, neither will He task a soul beyond its power.[6]

To the sincere ones, tests are as a gift from God, the Exalted, for a heroic person hasteneth, with the utmost joy and gladness, to the tests of a violent battlefield, but the coward is afraid and trembles and utters moaning and lamentation. Likewise, an expert student prepareth and memorizeth his lessons and exercises with the utmost effort, and in the day of examination he appeareth with infinite joy before the master.[7]

Remember not your own limitations; the help of God will come to you. Forget yourself. God's help will surely come![8]

Tests and trials are opportunities to learn, to become more mature. Each of us should ask ourselves: Am I willing to make the effort to learn, or do I try to avoid the problem? I may try to escape the problem by refusing to recognize it, by blaming others, or by making a half-hearted, unintelligent approach to it. If I succeed in avoiding the test it is likely to recur again and again, until I face it and solve it. The psychologist Alfred Adler wrote that the person who tries to avoid all problems is acting as though he wishes to 'live like a worm in an apple'!

How can we be happy in the face of problems which are due to our own weaknesses and errors? If you have lost your way in the woods, by taking the wrong turn when the path forked, you return to the fork, and are joyful to move forward on the path which will take you to your destination. Similarly, we can be happy in learning what we should *not* do in the future.

We should not waste our energy by dwelling on our failures. We should form the habit of looking for the cause of the error. Then, if we can do something to correct the mistake, let us do it at once. If we cannot repair the harm we have done, let us plan how we can do better to meet a similar situation next time it arises. We should then move ahead into constructive activity, rather than feel we are being 'noble' when we use time and energy in regret and remorse.

Worry is another emotion with which some people meet tests and problems. The dictionary defines 'to worry' as 'to torment oneself with, or suffer from, disturbing thoughts; to dwell uncomfortably on actual or possible troubles'. Worry, like remorse, is an unproductive use of time and energy. It is incompatible with an intelligent effort to solve the problem. If you worry about a difficult university entrance examination that you must take, you are wasting time which could be spent in study: you cannot worry and study at the same time. If you worry about the success of a public talk on the Bahá'í Faith which you are to give this evening, you are showing a lack of common sense: do you wish your mind to be a confused, unhappy turmoil when you address the audience? If you have prepared the talk to the best of your ability, leave its delivery in the hands of God, and go to a film, or read an interesting book.

When God sends us difficult problems we often cannot see their usefulness for our own development. I may be unhappy because the direction of my life seems to be deflected from what I thought was a fine and creative goal. I may feel that many of my most unselfish efforts have been wasted. But I can foresee only a small section of my life, on my way through eternity. God, who 'sees the end from the beginning', has for me a larger and more glorious goal than I can imagine. My faith in His goodness and justice must be so deep that I can rejoice in the methods He uses to educate me.

> ... the mesh of divine destiny exceedeth the vastest of mortal conceptions, and the dart of His decree transcendeth the boldest of human designs. None can escape the snares He setteth, and no soul can find release except through submission to His will.[9]

> Anybody can be happy in the state of comfort, ease, health, success, pleasure and joy; but if one will be happy and contented in the time of trouble, hardship and prevailing disease, it is the proof of nobility. . . .
> . . . Still, as the believers of God are turning to the limitless world, they do not become very depressed and sad by disastrous calamities — there is something to console them . . .[10]

Most of us at times have lived through a week or a month when problems piled up to an overwhelming extent. They may not be very difficult problems, but there seem to be far too many of them for our time and energy. Or one problem may be of such intensity and importance that we feel greatly burdened. We develop physical and emotional tensions which decrease our efficiency. This is a sign that we should look for a temporary escape from pressure. Each individual should try to find one or two activities which are excellent 'escape mechanisms' for him. Among these may be included playing or listening to music, singing, walking, swimming, reading detective stories or books of humour, going to a film, gardening, and talking with friends. The important consideration is that the activity 'takes one out of oneself', that one becomes completely 'lost' in it. The purpose of the escape is to enable one to return to one's problems refreshed, with renewed energy.

Bahá'u'lláh used to take His little granddaughters to the Riḍván garden for a picnic, and evidently found that their happiness refreshed Him. 'Abdu'l-Bahá, in His younger days, used to enjoy riding horseback, and at the end of a tiring day of travel, He told His followers many funny stories in order to relieve tensions. Both He and Bahá'u'lláh found re-creation in the beauty of trees and flowers and birds. Shoghi Effendi's love of gardens, Chinese art, and majestic architecture must have given him temporary release from the problems in human relations which filled so much of his life.

Do not feel that you are doing wrong when you make a brief, temporary escape from the problems and tests of life. Do not confuse this with the retreat of the person who continually avoids responsibilities and problems.

Respect the temporary escape techniques of others: if your tensions are released by playing the piano, realize that a detective story or a game of chess may serve the same purpose for others!

Illness and Accidents

Most of us have at some time been ill for days and weeks at a time, or we have been confined to the house because of a broken bone. We may have been in great pain, or prolonged inactivity may have caused tension and irritation. We may have been very disturbed because our illness placed extra burdens on others.

Great faith and courage are necessary if a person is to face illness and physical injury with inner tranquillity. At such times a Bahá'í has extra time for the study of the Bahá'í Writings, for prayer, and for some form of service to the Faith which does not require much physical activity. One man who was in hospital for months with a broken leg presented the teachings to all the men in his ward. A woman who was confined to the house with a heart attack spent her convalescence writing letters to pioneers in far corners of the earth.

If a person is in great pain the prayers of his friends may be his greatest solace.

'Abdu'l-Bahá once wrote to a Bahá'í, 'spiritual health is conducive to physical health.' Many illnesses of the body are caused by our lack of spiritual and emotional health. We can bring sickness on ourselves by our lack of spiritual maturity. 'Abdu'l-Bahá did not use the term 'psychosomatic illness', but He indicated clearly that illness may be the result of mistaken thinking and feeling.

> If we are caused joy or pain by a friend, if a love prove true or false, it is the soul that is affected. If our dear ones are far from us — it is the soul that grieves, and the grief or trouble of the soul may react on the body.[11]

Illness caused by physical accident should be treated with medical remedies; those which are due to spiritual causes disappear through spiritual means. Thus an illness caused by affliction, fear, nervous impressions, will be healed by spiritual rather than by physical treatment. Hence, both kinds of remedies should be considered.[12]

So when a sick person has a strong desire and intense hope for something, and hears suddenly the tidings of its realization, a nervous excitement is produced, which will make the malady entirely disappear.[13]

Fear, worry, anger, hatred, and lust for power over others are indications of spiritual immaturity. All of them may become causes of physical as well as mental illness. A high proportion of accidents are due to carelessness, recklessness, or poor judgement. All of these can be prevented.

As mankind develops greater spiritual maturity and becomes more thoughtful about others, illnesses and accidents will decrease. Now we must do all that we can, not only to maintain our own health, but also to protect the health and safety of others. The Bahá'í who develps inner spiritual tranquillity, through faith in God and His Divine Educators, need not be afflicted by psychosomatic illness, nor be 'accident prone'.

Send down, then, upon them that which will assure their hearts, and quiet their souls, and renew their spirits, and refresh their bodies.[14]

A Bahá'í uses, to heal himself and others, prayers

which were revealed by Bahá'u'lláh and 'Abdu'l-Bahá. He believes that these inspired words release spiritual forces which heal and calm the one who is ill. The following lines by Bahá'u'lláh illustrate how physical, mental and spiritual illnesses are all considered in Bahá'í healing prayers:

> Thou art He, O my God, through Whose names the sick are healed and the ailing are restored, and the thirsty are given drink, and the sore-vexed are tranquillized, and the wayward are guided, and the abased are exalted, and the poor are enriched, and the ignorant are enlightened, and the gloomy are illumined, and the sorrowful are cheered, and the chilled are warmed, and the downtrodden are raised up. . . . [15]

When We Grow Older

Robert Browning begins his poem, 'Rabbi Ben Ezra', with these words:

> Grow old along with me!
> The best is yet to be,
> The last of life, for which the first was made:
> Our times are in his hand
> Who saith, 'A whole I planned,
> Youth shows but half; trust God: see all, nor be
> afraid!'

This is a joyful approach to old age, and is the necessary result of an earlier life which has been mature in outlook and action.

As we grow older our physical energy gradually

decreases; our sense organs may function less accurately; we may require more assistance from others; we probably have less money to spend. These are disadvantages which we have to accept, and we should try to accept them with 'radiant acquiescence'.

What are the advantages of growing older? We have a fund of experience and knowledge which the young person does not, and we can use this to solve our own problems and, sometimes, to help others. We have developed habits of friendliness and unselfishness which bring joy to others. We have achieved a deep spiritual tranquillity which frees us from emotional storm and stress. We have become more certain that God's plan for us is good. We may have all of these advantages if we have worked towards them earlier in our lives.

The Bahá'í Writings contain comparatively little that is specifically related to the way we should meet old age. This suggests that, if we have conscientiously lived by the teachings, old age need not be a serious problem. If, year by year, we have used the intelligence God has given, our thinking in old age should be better than ever before. (In certain diseases of old age the mind ceases to function well, but we do not know the extent to which these are psychosomatic in origin, and so could have been prevented.)

If the aged govern their actions by consideration for others and by trust in God, they will be a help, rather than a hindrance, to family and friends. The older person should use imagination to judge how others feel about his behaviour. There are some actions which, at all ages, are disturbing to others, but which may be more common in the aged. The following list suggests some of the kinds of behaviour which older people should avoid.

1. Do not complain frequently about loss of physical strength. Do all you can to keep yourself in good health, and accept your physical limitations gracefully.

2. Do not refuse assistance in your physical activities when you really need it. If you need help in going up a flight of stairs, ask for it in a matter-of-fact way. If you cannot carry a heavy object which has to be moved, ask a friend to do it for you.

3. Do not refuse financial assistance when you really need it. To say, 'I am too proud to accept money', shows a lack of consideration for the helpfulness others would like to show. Of course you must not use gifts or loans extravagantly.

4. Do not burden others unnecessarily. If you are so deaf that you need a hearing aid, buy one (if you can afford it), and then *use* it. If you have such an aid and do not use it because you 'don't like it', you are being inconsiderate to those who wish to talk with you.

5. Do not become careless with regard to the neatness and cleanliness of your body and your clothing. If your physical control is poor and you get spots on your suit, clean them off as soon as possible!

6. Never complain and whine about things you don't like. The person who frequently has 'hurt feelings' is a nuisance at any age. If you are elderly and often get your feelings hurt, you are implying that others are purposely being unkind. Among Bahá'ís this will certainly not be true. You must assume that the intentions of others are friendly.

7. Do not expect younger people to conform to the social conventions of *your* youth. Do not tell them that the gay sports shirt, or the purple pyjamas are in bad taste. Accept the fact that conventions in clothing and behaviour do change, and that many of these changes have nothing to do with moral values.

8. Avoid saying, 'When you are as old as I am, you will see how mistaken you are.' Younger people need to learn their own lessons. If you have a helpful idea, put it forward as a suggestion, but do not imply that your age gives you a right to dictate to others. Remember that the ideas of the aged are not *necessarily* better than those of youth.

9. Guard against frequent repetition of a suggestion, a fact, or a story. I heard an elderly mother say to her fifty-year-old daughter, 'You'd better take your galoshes; it looks like rain.' Three or four minutes later she said, 'Alice, take your galoshes: it's going to rain.' And again, as her daughter started for her car, 'Alice, you haven't your galoshes. Wait till I get them for you.'

If you have a good story about the big fish you caught thirty years ago, but cannot remember whether you have told it to a particular group, start to tell it and watch the listeners' faces. When they have heard it their facial expressions will usually show it, sometimes by a polite blankness. If so, stop and say, 'Yes I remember now, I've told you that one. I'd like to hear some of *your* stories.'

10. Do not expect younger people to amuse and entertain you. They have their own work to do. If you have lived a full and active life up to the age of sixty-five or seventy, you probably have many things you want to do when you retire from a full-time job. A man of sixty-five first painted his own house, and then found himself in demand for painting and repairing the homes of elderly widows in his church. A retired business executive began to take piano lessons, and discovered that he had unsuspected ability in the field of music. After a year of work he had developed skill which made his playing a delight to all his friends. Use imagination in gaining new knowledge and abilities which give help and joy to others, as well as to yourself.

Older Bahá'ís who have retired from business or a profession can always find work to do for the Faith. One woman of seventy who lived in a home for the aged spent many hours transcribing some of the Bahá'í Writings into Braille. Many older people whose income would have been inadequate in the United States have gone as Bahá'í teachers to far-away places, and have found that they can live comfortably and still have money to contribute to the work of the

Faith. Others, in their home communities, act as hostesses and librarians at Bahá'í centres, or look after children so that mothers may attend a class.

Note that each of the above 'Don'ts' has been followed by a 'Do!' Each of the latter implies consideration for the welfare and happiness of others. What more can one expect to achieve, at any age? If younger people forget how old you are and treat you as one of themselves, consider this a compliment, and an indication that you have not been seeking special privileges.

Many elderly people say, 'I do not *feel* old. It is hard for me to realize how old I am.' Younger people should encourage this attitude and, whenever possible, accept the aged into a human fellowship which disregards age.

Give older people the assistance, physical or financial, which they feel they need, but do not give more, even though you think they need it. (Of course there are exceptions to this advice, if the older person is mentally incompetent.) Mrs. B., a frail woman of eighty, wished to go on an all-day trip by car on a bitterly cold day. The driver of the car refused to take her, on the grounds that it would tire her too much. So Mrs. B. spent the day at home alone, unhappy in the feeling that her friends did not want her with them. Undoubtedly the trip would have tired her, but the fatigue would have been easy to bear in comparison with the feeling that she was not wanted by those she loved.

Members of the family of an aged person should not discuss the latter's health and physical disabilities with others in the presence of the older man or woman. Make every effort to protect the elderly from losing face; do not make them feel that they are being treated as children.

The older person sometimes becomes much slower in movement and therefore seems to take too much time in carrying out simple activities. Be patient with his slowness, realizing that it may be a comparatively few years before *you* will 'slow down'.

Some old people may make unreasonable demands on your time and energy. To give in to such demands is a mistaken kindness. Refuse pleasantly, but definitely, and do not feel guilty in doing so. It is possible to learn new attitudes and habits after one is seventy or eighty, and if a man or woman has not learned consideration for others earlier, he can start when he is old. Certainly, younger people should not encourage him in unreasonable demands.

If younger and older people love one another and make a real effort to be understanding, the association can be one of happiness and spiritual growth for all of them.

'I Have Made Death a Messenger of Joy to Thee'

As a child of seven or eight years I had a great fear of death. I thought a great deal about how I could avoid it, and finally decided that the best thing to do was to pray ardently that Christ would come again during my lifetime. I understood, from the teaching I had received in Sunday school, that when He came we would all be 'caught up into Heaven' with Him. If this could happen to me I could avoid dying!

I cannot remember why I feared death so much, but the fear was probably related to one or more of the following common reasons:

1. Some people dread dying because they fear punishment for wrongdoing. The religions of millions teach them that they will, after death, go to hell because of their shortcomings and sins, unless they have received ritual purification and forgiveness.

2. Others are terrified of the unknown world which they believe lies beyond death. They think, 'We know what this present world is like. Even though our life here is unhappy, it is probably better than the unknown darkness of death.' Those who find this life good are unwilling to lose its pleasures. 'We cannot be sure that the next life will have anything to compensate us for what we are losing.'

3. A man may feel that he has no self, no identity, apart from his body. He is not especially concerned about giving up the joys and pleasures of this earth, but he has a great dread of losing his very self when his body is destroyed by death. Often he is not actively conscious of this aspect of his fear of dying, but it is even more terrifying if it looms darkly below the level of consciousness. This fear of losing one's very self at death is much more common than most people

suppose.

Assurance of the immortality of the individual human spirit can be achieved only through an act of faith. I cannot 'prove' to you that the very essence of your self — your spirit — will continue, after the death of your body, through the eternal kingdom for evermore. But if you have accepted, without reservation, one of the great Manifestations of God as your guide and teacher, your faith in His Divine Word will gradually free you from the fear of the loss of your body. Moreover, this faith will lead you to look forward joyfully to an existence in the 'glorious heights' of eternity.

This faith and assurance comes to Bahá'ís from meditation on passages such as the following from *The Hidden Words* of Bahá'u'lláh.

> O Son of Man! Thou art My dominion and My dominion perisheth not, wherefore fearest thou thy perishing? Thou art My light and My light shall never be extinguished, why dost thou dread extinction? Thou art My glory and My glory fadeth not; thou art My robe and My robe shall never be outworn. Abide then in thy love for Me, that thou mayest find Me in the realm of glory.[16]

> O Son of the Supreme! I have made death a messenger of joy to thee. Wherefore dost thou grieve? I made the light to shed on thee its splendour. Why dost thou veil thyself therefrom?[17]

> O Son of Love! Thou art but one step away from the glorious heights above and from the celestial tree of love. Take thou one pace and with

the next advance into the immortal realm and enter the pavilion of eternity. Give ear then to that which hath been revealed by the pen of glory.[18]

O Companion of My Throne! . . . Live then the days of thy life, that are less than a fleeting moment, with thy mind stainless, thy heart unsullied, thy thoughts pure, and thy nature sanctified, so that, free and content, thou mayest put away this mortal frame, and repair unto the mystic paradise and abide in the eternal kingdom for evermore.[19]

When you have acquired a deep inner conviction that you will continue to live through the unthinkable ages of eternity, you can begin to live in the eternal kingdom while still on this earth. You will be less impatient when God's plan seems to be unfolding slowly. When you have tried your best, but a certain plan has not succeeded in increasing the welfare of others, you will be able to accept this apparent failure with tranquillity, knowing that if the plan was good, what you tried to do will eventually come to pass. You will have more understanding of the slow development of some people, and will have faith in their ultimate maturing.

This effort to live in eternity, here and now, is a true preparation for the death of the body, which you will welcome as a 'messenger of joy'.

Be a Joy Bringer

A Bahá'í should bring joy and tranquillity to every person he meets.

... bestow abundant effort in rejoicing the
souls.[20]

Be thou loving to every afflicted one, a dis-
peller of sorrows to every grieved one, ... a
consolation to dejected hearts, ... a succour to
every lamenting one ... [21]

In almost every chapter of this book we have
discussed the attitudes and actions which bring happiness to others. 'Abdu'l-Bahá always sympathized
with the sorrows and difficulties of those who sought
Him for help and comfort. But He discouraged them
from brooding on these experiences. To a Bahá'í who
had suffered a serious financial loss He wrote:

Do not feel sorry; do not brood over the loss;
do not sit down depressed; do not be silent ... [22]

To Sarah Farmer, whose much-loved home had
been destroyed by fire, He said:

Be not grieved if the trash of the world is
decreased in thy hands. . .[23]

To a mother whose young daughter had died He
wrote:

Be calm, be strong, be grateful, and become a
lamp full of light, that the darkness of sorrows be
annihilated, and that the sun of everlasting joy
arise from the dawning-place of heart and soul,
shining brightly.[24]

From the above quotations it is clear that our sympathy and understanding must increase rather than decrease the spiritual maturity of those whose lives touch ours. We should not encourage others in a negative acceptance of life's difficulties; instead we must help them to achieve a positive, active happiness.

We shall bring joy and peace to others only to the extent that we love them unselfishly, and only as long as our own lives mirror forth the characteristics of God.

*   *   *

'O Thou kind Lord! O Thou Who art generous and merciful! We are the servants of Thy threshold and are gathered beneath the sheltering shadow of Thy divine unity. The sun of Thy mercy is shining upon all, and the clouds of Thy bounty shower upon all. Thy gifts encompass all, Thy loving providence sustains all, Thy protection overshadows all, and the glances of Thy favour are cast upon all. O Lord! Grant Thine infinite bestowals, and let the light of Thy guidance shine. Illumine the eyes, gladden the hearts with abiding joy. Confer a new spirit upon all people and bestow upon them eternal life. Unlock the gates of true understanding and let the light of faith shine resplendent. Gather all people beneath the shadow of Thy bounty and cause them to unite in harmony, so that they may become as the rays of one sun, as the waves of one ocean, and as the fruit of one tree. May they drink from the same fountain. May they be refreshed by the same breeze. May they receive illumination from the same source of light. Thou art the Giver, the Merciful, the Omnipotent.'

'Abdu'l-Bahá

BIBLIOGRAPHY

Bahá'í Administration: Shoghi Effendi. Wilmette, Illinois; Bahá'í Publishing Committee, 1928, 5th edn. 1945.

Bahá'í Prayers: A Selection. London; Bahá'í Publishing Trust, 1945, 4th edn. 1975.

Bahá'í Procedure: Shoghi Effendi. Wilmette, Illinois; Bahá'í Publishing Committee, 1942.

Bahá'í World, The: An International Record. Vol. 2, 1926-1928. New York; Bahá'í Publishing Committee, 1928.

Bahá'í World Faith: Selected Writings of Bahá'u'lláh and 'Abdu'l-Bahá. Wilmette, Illinois; Bahá'í Publishing Trust, 1943, 2nd edn. 1956, reprinted 1976.

Bahá'u'lláh and the New Era: J. E. Esslemont. First published 1923, London; Bahá'í Publishing Trust, 4th edn. 1974.

Chosen Highway, The: Lady Blomfield. First published London, 1940. Wilmette, Illinois; Bahá'í Publishing Trust, 1967.

Daryáy-i-Dánish: Bahá'u'lláh. New Delhi: Bahá'í Publishing Trust.

Dawn-Breakers, The: Nabíl's Narrative of the Early Days of the Bahá'í Revelation. Wilmette, Illinois; Bahá'í Publishing Trust, 1932, reprinted 1974.

Epistle to the Son of the Wolf: Bahá'u'lláh, translated by Shoghi Effendi. Wilmette, Illinois; Bahá'í Publishing Trust, 1941, 2nd edn. 1953, reprinted 1976.

Gleanings from the Writings of Bahá'u'lláh: translated by Shoghi Effendi. Wilmette, Illinois; Bahá'í Publishing Trust, 1939, 3rd edn. 1976.

Hidden Words, The: Bahá'u'lláh, translated by Shoghi Effendi with the assistance of some English friends. London; Bahá'í Publishing Trust, 1932, reprinted 1975.

Kitáb-i-Íqán, The: Bahá'u'lláh. The Book of Certitude, translated by Shoghi Effendi. London; Bahá'í Publishing Trust, 1946, 2nd edn. 1961.

Lifeblood of the Cause: A compilation of extracts from the letters of Shoghi Effendi issued by the Universal House of Justice. Oakham, England; Bahá'í Publishing Trust, 1970.

Oriental Rose, The: Mary Hanford Ford. New York; Broadway Publishing Co., 1910.

Paris Talks: Addresses given by 'Abdu'l-Bahá in Paris in 1911-12. First published 1912. London; Bahá'í Publishing Trust, 11th British edn. 1969, reprinted 1972. (Published as *The Wisdom of 'Abdu'l-Bahá* in the U.S.A.)

Prayers and Meditations by Bahá'u'lláh: translated by Shoghi Effendi. Wilmette, Illinois; Bahá'í Publishing Trust, 1938, reprinted 1974.

Promulgation of Universal Peace, The: Discourses by Abdul Baha Abbas During His Visit to the United States in 1912. Vol. 1, Chicago; Executive Board of Bahai Temple Unity, 1922. Vol. 2, Chicago; Bahai Publishing Committee, 1925. Published complete in one volume, Wilmette, Illinois; Bahai Publishing Committee, 1943.

Secret of Divine Civilization, The: 'Abdu'l-Bahá, translated by Marzieh Gail. Wilmette, Illinois; Bahá'í Publishing Trust, 1957, 2nd edn. 1970, reprinted 1975.

Some Answered Questions: Collected and Translated from the Persian of 'Abdu'l-Bahá by Laura Clifford Barney. First published London, 1908. Wilmette, Illinois; Bahá'í Publishing Trust, 7th edn. 1954.

Star of the West: Vols. 7, 9, 11. Chicago; The Bahai News Service, 1916, 1918, 1920. Reprinted, in vols. 4, 5, 6. Oxford; George Ronald, 1978.

Tablets of Abdul-Baha Abbas: 3 volumes. First published 1909-16. New York; Bahá'í Publishing Committee, 1930.

Tablets of Bahá'u'lláh: Compiled by the Research Department of the Universal House of Justice and translated by Habib Taherzadeh with the assistance of a Committee at the Bahá'í World Centre. Haifa; Bahá'í World Centre, 1978.

REFERENCES

For full titles of the books referred to, as well as for names of authors and other details, please refer to the Bibliography. If authorship is in doubt, the name is given in the reference. In the list of references, the page number is that of the last edition shown in the Bibliography; *Tablets* refers to *Tablets of Abdul-Baha Abbas.*

1.   WHY THIS BOOK?

1. *Tablets,* vol. 2, pp.306-7
2. *Promulgation,* Introduction, p.i
3. *Tablets of Bahá'u'lláh,* p. 36
4. *Gleanings,* CXXXI, p. 287

2. THE PRISON OF SELF

1. *Hidden Words,* Arabic, no. 68
2. *Hidden Words,* Persian, no. 40
3. *Hidden Words,* Persian, no. 72
4. *Tablets,* vol. 3, p. 722
5. *Tablets,* vol. 1, p. 136
6. *Gleanings,* CXLV, p. 315
7. *Gleanings,* V, p. 8
8. *Tablets,* vol. 3, p. 663
9. *Secret of Divine Civilization,* p. 39
10. *Epistle to the Son of the Wolf,* p. 94
11. *Hidden Words,* Persian, no. 6
12. *Secret of Divine Civilization,* p. 6
13. *Hidden Words,* Arabic, no. 26
14. *Hidden Words,* Persian, no. 66
15. *Tablets,* vol. 1, p. 45
16. *Promulgation,* p. 89
17. *Kitáb-i-Íqán,* p. 124; (U.S. edn., p. 193-4)
18. *Hidden Words,* Persian, no. 44
19. *Gleanings,* CXXV, p. 265
20. *Hidden Words,* Persian, no. 5
21. *Tablets,* vol. 1, p. 133
22. *Epistle to the Son of the Wolf,* p. 93
23. *Kitáb-i-Íqán,* p. 124; (U.S. edn., p. 194)
24. *Tablets,* vol. 1, p. 42
25. *Promulgation,* p. 60
26. *Bahá'í Administration,* p.22, from 'Abdu'l-Bahá

Prayer: *Bahá'í Prayers,* no. 100, p. 105

3. STRIVE FOR GENTLENESS AND LOVE

1. *Promulgation,* p. 60
2. *Tablets,* vol. 3, p. 657
3. *Promulgation,* p. 124
4. *Epistle to the Son of the Wolf,* p. 93
5. *Promulgation,* p. 6

6.   *Tablets*, vol. 2, p. 244
7.   *Paris Talks*, pp. 95-6 ('The Desires and Prayers . . .')
8.   *Promulgation*, p. 213
9.   *Star*, Vol. 11, no. 1 (March 1920), p. 20
10. *Paris Talks*, p. 15 ('The Duty of Kindness . . .')
11. *Tablets*, vol. 1, p. 43
12. *Tablets*, vol. 2, p. 389
13. *Promulgation*, p. 199
14. *Bahá'í World*, vol. 2, p. 50, from 'Abdu'l-Bahá
15. *Paris Talks*, p. 179 ('The Four Kinds of Love')
16. *Promulgation*, p. 13
17. *Tablets*, vol. 3, p. 505
18. *Some Answered Questions*, pp. 345-6, ch. LXXXIV
19. *Promulgation*, p. 226
20. *Paris Talks*, p. 38 ('The Universal Love')
21. *Paris Talks*, p. 37 ('The Universal Love')
22. *Promulgation*, p. 316

4.   ACTION AND ACHIEVEMENT

1.   *Promulgation*, p. 86
2.   *Tablets of Baha'u'llah*, p. 156
3.   *Paris Talks*, pp. 176-7 ('Prayer as Service')
4.   *Paris Talks*, p 16 ('The Duty of Kindness . . .')
5.   *Secret of Divine Civilization*, p.34
6.   *Secret of Divine Civilization*, p. 108
7.   *Chosen Highway*, p. 177
8.   *Paris Talks*, p. 39 ('The Universal Love')
9.   *Promulgation*, p. 152
10. *Tablets*, vol. 3, p. 691
11. *Paris Talks*, pp. 80-1 ('Good Ideas Must be Carried . . .')
12. *Some Answered Questions*, p. 287, ch. LXX
13. *Gleanings*, XXXIV, pp. 81-2
14. *Secret of Divine Civilization*, p.66
15. *Tablets*, vol. 2, p. 265
16. *Tablets*, vol. 2, p. 458

17. *Gleanings*, LXXVII, p. 149
18. *Paris Talks*, p. 81 ('Good Ideas Must Be Carried . . .')

5. THE USE OF INTELLIGENCE

1. *Paris Talks*, p. 69 ('The Two Kinds of Light')
2. *Promulgation*, p. 47
3. *Promulgation*, p. 60
4. *Promulgation*, p. 63
5. *Gleanings*, XCV, p. 194
6. *Paris Talks,* pp. 41-2 ('God's Greatest Gift . . .')
7. *Some Answered Questions*, p. 252, ch. LVIII
8. *Promulgation*, p. 176
9. *Paris Talks*, p. 90 ('The Evolution of the Spirit')
10. *Promulgation*, p. 59
11. *Paris Talks*, pp. 136-7 ('The First Principle . . .')
12. *Promulgation*, p. 47
13. *Promulgation*, p. 103
14. *Promulgation*, p. 139
15. *Promulgation*, p. 226
16. *Paris Talks*, p. 143 ('Fourth Principle . . .')
17. *Gleanings*, CXX, p. 255
18. *Some Answered Questions*, p. 200, ch. XLV
19. *Gleanings*, LXX, p. 136
Prayer: *Bahá'í Prayers*, no. 69, pp. 75-6

6. THE USE OF MONEY

1. *Tablets of Bahá'u'lláh*, p. 26
2. *Hidden Words*, Persian, no. 80
3. *Hidden Words*, Persian, no. 82
4. *Gleanings*, CXXVIII, p. 276
5. *Bahá'í World Faith*, p. 375, from 'Abdu'l-Bahá
6. *Tablets*, vol. 2, p. 294
7. *Tablets of Bahá'u'lláh*, p. 23
8. *Gleanings*, CXVIII, p. 251
9. *Gleanings,* CXIV, p. 235

10. *Bahá'í World Faith*, p. 62
11. *Oriental Rose*, p. 165
12. *Gleanings*, CXIV, p. 235
13. *Tablets of Bahá'u'lláh*, p. 38
14. *Epistle to the Son of the Wolf*, p. 55
15. *Epistle to the Son of the Wolf*, p. 93
16. *Tablets*, vol. 1, p. 37
17. *Promulgation*, p. 211
18. *Secret of Divine Civilization*, p. 24
19. *Bahá'í Procedure*, p. 9 and *Lifeblood of the Cause*, p. 12
20. *Bahá'í Procedure*, p. 9 and *Lifeblood of the Cause*, p. 12
21. *Bahá'í Procedure*, p. 20, from Shoghi Effendi
Prayer: *Bahá'í Prayers*, no. 86, pp. 89-90

7.   THE DEVELOPMENT OF ARTS AND SCIENCES

1. *Daryáy-i-Dánish*, p. 106
2. *Tablets of Bahá'u'lláh*, p. 52
3. *Some Answered Questions*, p. 157, ch. XXXIV
4. *Bahá'í World Faith*, p. 377 from 'Abdu'l-Bahá
5. *Gleanings*, LXXIV, pp. 141-2
6. *Gleanings*, LXXXII, p. 161
7. *Tablets of Bahá'u'lláh*, p. 72
8. *Promulgation*, p. 48
9. *Promulgation*, p. 46
10. *Promulgation*, pp. 46-7

8.   EDUCATION IN THE HOME

1. *Epistle to the Son of the Wolf*, pp. 26-7
2. *Tablets of Bahá'u'lláh*, p. 90
3. *Tablets of Bahá'u'lláh*, p. 68
4. *Some Answered Questions*, p. 156, ch. XXXIV
5. *Some Answered Questions*, p. 9, ch. III
6. *Tablets*, vol. 3, pp. 578-80
7. *Promulgation*, p. 136
8. *Some Answered Questions*, p. 249, ch. LVII

9.   *Tablets of Bahá'u'lláh*, p. 88
10.   *Epistle to the Son of the Wolf*, p. 50
11.   *Promulgation*, p. 163
12.   *Promulgation*, pp. 175-6
13.   *Promulgation*, p. 51
14.   *Gleanings*, CXXXVI, p. 295
15.   *Gleanings*, CXII, p. 219
16.   *Star*, vol. 7, no. 15 (Dec. 1916), p. 142, from 'Abdu'l-Bahá
17.   *Bahá'í World Faith*, p. 374, from 'Abdu'l-Bahá

9.   EDUCATION IN SCHOOLS

1.   *Bahá'í World Faith*, p. 398, from 'Abdu'l-Bahá
2.   *Star*, vol. 9, no. 8 (Aug. 1918), p. 89, from 'Abdu'l-Bahá
3.   *Bahá'í World Faith*, pp. 397-8, from 'Abdu'l-Bahá
4.   *Promulgation* p. 104
5.   *Promulgation*, p. 73
6.   *Star*, vol. 7, no. 15 (Dec. 1916), p. 142, from 'Abdu'l-Bahá
7.   *Promulgation*, pp. 49-50
8.   *Tablets*, vol. 3, p. 501
9.   *Tablets*, vol. 3, p. 546
10.   *Dawn-Breakers*, pp. 258-9; (U.K. edn., p. 181)
11.   *Tablets of Bahá'u'lláh*, p. 22
12.   *Tablets of Bahá'u'lláh*, p. 68
13.   *Paris Talks*, p. 156 ('The Eighth Principle . . .')
14.   *Some Answered Questions*, p. 274, ch. LXIV
15.   *Paris Talks*, p. 43 ('God's Greatest Gift . . .')
16.   *Paris Talks*, p. 137 ('The First Principle . . .')
17.   *Secret of Divine Civilization*, p. 106
18.   *Gleanings*, CXXII, p. 260

10.   MEN AND WOMEN

1.   *Promulgation*, p. 161
2.   *Paris Talks*, p. 162 ('The Tenth Principle . . .')
3.   *Promulgation*, p. 177
4.   *Promulgation*, p. 73

5. *Promulgation*, p. 104
6. *Paris Talks,* p. 162 ('The Tenth Principle . . .')
7. *Bahá'í World Faith,* p. 372, from 'Abdu'l-Bahá
8. *Tablets*, vol. 3, pp. 605-6
9. *Star,* vol. 11, no. 1 (March 1920), p. 20-1
10. *Baha'u'llah and the New Era*, p.164, ch.11 ('Marriage'), from Bahá'u'lláh
11. *Tablets*, vol. 3, p. 563
12. *Bahá'í World Faith,* p. 372, from 'Abdu'l-Bahá
13. *Bahá'u'lláh and the New Era,* p. 165, ch. 11 ('Divorce')
Prayer: *Bahá'í Prayers*, Special Occasions, p. 46

11.   FAIRNESS TO YOURSELF AND OTHERS

1. *Gleanings*, CXXVIII, p. 278
2. *Secret of Divine Civilization*, p. 39
3. *Hidden Words*, Arabic, no. 2
4. *Gleanings*, CLXIII, p. 342
5. *Bahá'í World Faith*, p. 180
6. *Gleanings*, LXVI, p. 128
7. *Gleanings*, C, p. 204
8. *Hidden Words*, Persian, no. 43
9. *Promulgation*, p. 177
10. *Paris Talks,* p. 159 ('Ninth Principle . . .')
11. *Paris Talks,* p. 154 ('Seventh Principle . . .')
12. *Paris Talks,* p. 154 ('Seventh Principle . . .')
13. *Paris Talks,* pp. 148-9 ('The Fifth Principle . . .')
14. *Promulgation*, p. 211
15. *Gleanings*, CXII, p. 219

12.   CONSULTATION

1. *Tablets of Bahá'u'lláh,* p. 126
2. *Promulgation*, p. 69
3. *Bahá'í Administration*, p. 22, from 'Abdu'l-Bahá
4. *Promulgation*, p. 69
5. *Tablets of Bahá'u'lláh,* p. 69

6. *Bahá'í Administration*, p. 21, from 'Abdu'l'Bahá
7. *Promulgation*, p. 178
Prayer: *Bahá'í Prayers*, no. 59, p. 61

13.   JOY GIVES US WINGS

1. *Oriental Rose*, pp. 211-12
2. *Hidden Words*, Arabic, no. 36
3. *Paris Talks,* pp. 111-12 ('Pain and Sorrow')
4. *Paris Talks,* pp. 109-10 ('Pain and Sorrow')
5. *Promulgation*, p. 183
6. *Gleanings*, LII, p. 106
7. *Bahá'í World Faith*, p. 371, from 'Abdu'l-Bahá
8. *Paris Talks*, p. 38 ('The Universal Love')
9. *Kitáb-i-Íqán*, p. 160; (U.S. edn, p. 251)
10. *Tablets*, vol. 2, pp. 263-4
11. *Paris Talks*, p. 65 ('The Evolution of Matter . . .')
12. *Tablets*, vol. 3, p. 587
13. *Some Answered Questions*, p. 294, ch. LXXII
14. *Prayers and Meditations,* p. 170, no. 101
15. *Prayers and Meditations,* p. 236, no. 147
16. *Hidden Words*, Arabic, no. 14
17. *Hidden Words*, Arabic, no. 32
18. *Hidden Words*, Persian, no. 7
19. *Hidden Words*, Persian, no. 44
20. *Tablets*, vol. 1, p. 37
21. *Tablets*, vol. 1, p. 202
22. *Tablets*, vol. 1, p. 133
23. *Tablets*, vol. 2, p. 294
24. *Tablets*, vol. 2, p. 405
Prayer: *Bahá'í Prayers*, no. 88, p. 91